Chopin Revisited for Piano

A New Perspective on Chopin Classics

Bryce Russell

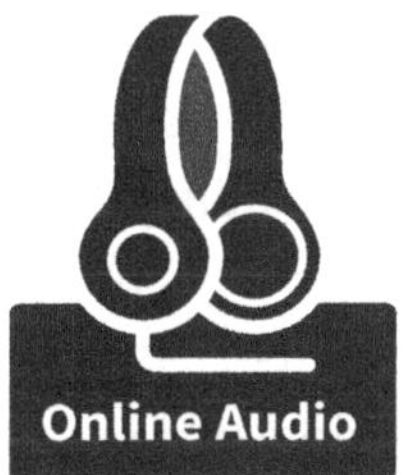

To access the online audio, scan the QR code above or go to:

www.melbay.com/31219MEB

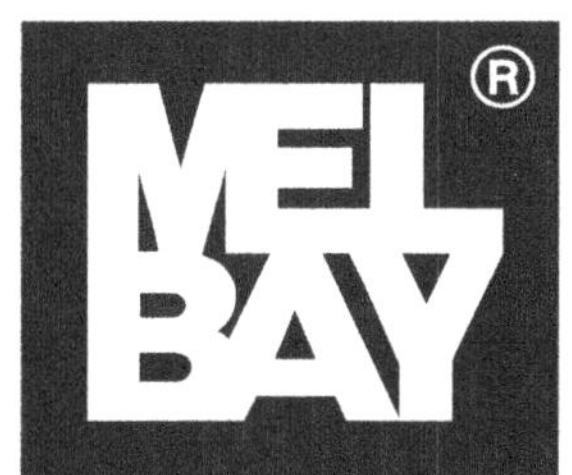

www.melbay.com

Preface

This varied collection contains twelve of Frédéric Chopin's very popular pieces arranged in the style of Jazz, and will be a unique perspective guaranteed to put a smile on musicians, students, teachers, and audiences everywhere. Included are some of the easier Mazurkas, Preludes, Waltzes, and one Nocturne. These pieces are a range of difficulty levels, and they have been left in their original keys to make them familiar to players and listeners. The rhythms were left intact as well, but with added Jazz harmonies built around Chopin's melodic gift. A few measures in some of the arrangements employ enharmonic spellings, this was an effort to maintain Chopin's original notation, but some notes/chords were notated differently for the sake of easier reading with fewer double flats and sharps.

Different interpretations of performance exist around Chopin's music, so a range of suggested tempo indications have been given, which should give an approximate rendition of each piece. However, since these arrangements are a twist on Chopin's music, the supplied audio/recordings will give the rendition that the arranger was trying to accomplish. No pedal indications have been given, this was intentional as you are free to employ pedaling at your own discretion.

To help with performance, I will provide a few comments on some key pieces in the collection. The *Mazurka in C Major Op. 67, No. 3* requires a light rubato, not too exaggerated, but somewhat quaint. The added descending bass line (mm. 1-4) is important in this arrangement, because it is built around a chromatic chord progression built on these chords of CMaj7, Bm7, B♭7, and Am7, which will be found throughout the arrangement. The *Mazurka in G♯ Minor Op. 33, No. 1* looks more difficult than it actually is, the piece is played pretty slow, roughly an Andante or Adagio tempo. Take your time with the note reading, because once the notation has been mastered, it will be easy to play. The *Nocturne in E♭ Major Op. 9, No. 2* is probably the most challenging piece in the collection, the notation makes it look more difficult than it actually is, but once again, it's played with an Andante tempo indication. So, take your time, and play the piece slower if necessary. The cadenza near the end can be played at any tempo you want.

The *Waltz in A♭ Major (L'adieu) Op. 69, No. 1* begins with a Lento tempo indication, however, make sure to maintain its waltz quality and not be too slow. At measure 33 it states "Con anima" which means the tempo should be increased in speed, but not too fast for this arrangement. Finally, the last piece for discussion, which is the *Waltz in B Minor Op. 69, No. 2.* This piece has variations of a chromatic scale in the right hand, the realized fingering given in the book is one method, but can be changed at will since there are many possibilities of playing these passages, see what works for you personally. You can use the advice given for these pieces can apply to the rest of the collection.

Enjoy this new Jazz perspective on Chopin's beautiful and dreamy music. I would like to thank all my friends and family for the support over the years, and another thanks goes to the fantastic staff at Mel Bay Publications. Without everyone's support this series would not be possible. Thank you!

Bryce Russell

Bryce Russell

Contents

Title	Page	Audio
Mazurka in A♭ Major Op. 24, No. 3	4	1
Mazurka in A Minor Op. 67, No. 4	6	2
Mazurka in C Major Op. 67, No. 3	10	3
Mazurka in F Major Op. 68, No. 3	14	4
Mazurka in G Minor Op. 67, No. 2	18	5
Mazurka in G♯ Minor Op. 33, No. 1	22	6
Prelude in A Major Op. 28, No. 7	25	7
Prelude in E Minor Op. 28, No. 4	26	8
Nocturne in E♭ Major Op. 9, No. 2	28	9
Waltz in A♭ Major (L'adieu) Op. 69, No. 1	32	10
Waltz in A Minor, Posthumous	38	11
Waltz in B Minor Op. 69, No. 2	42	12

Mazurka in A♭ Major

Op. 24, No. 3

Frédéric Chopin

Arranged by Bryce Russell

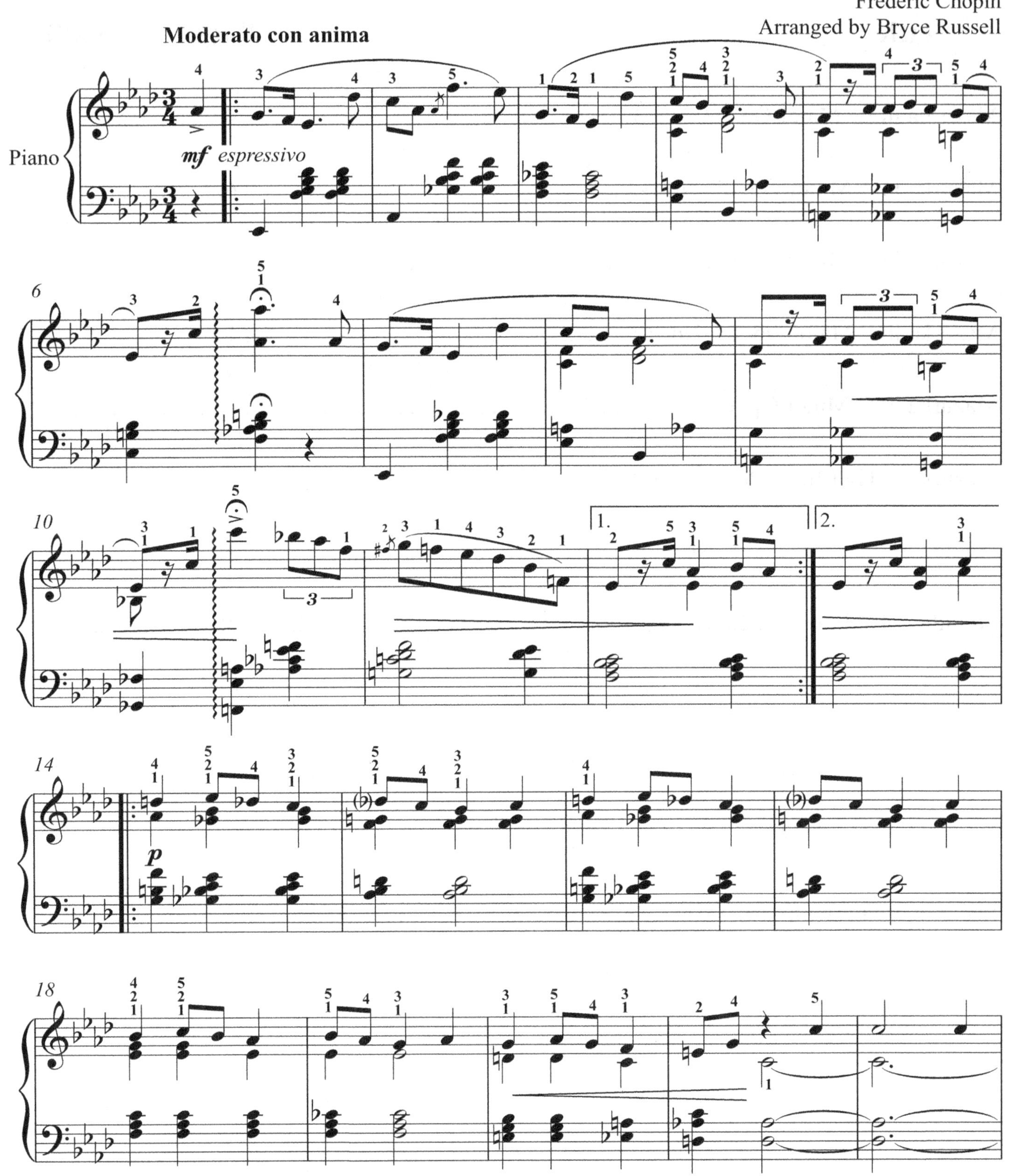

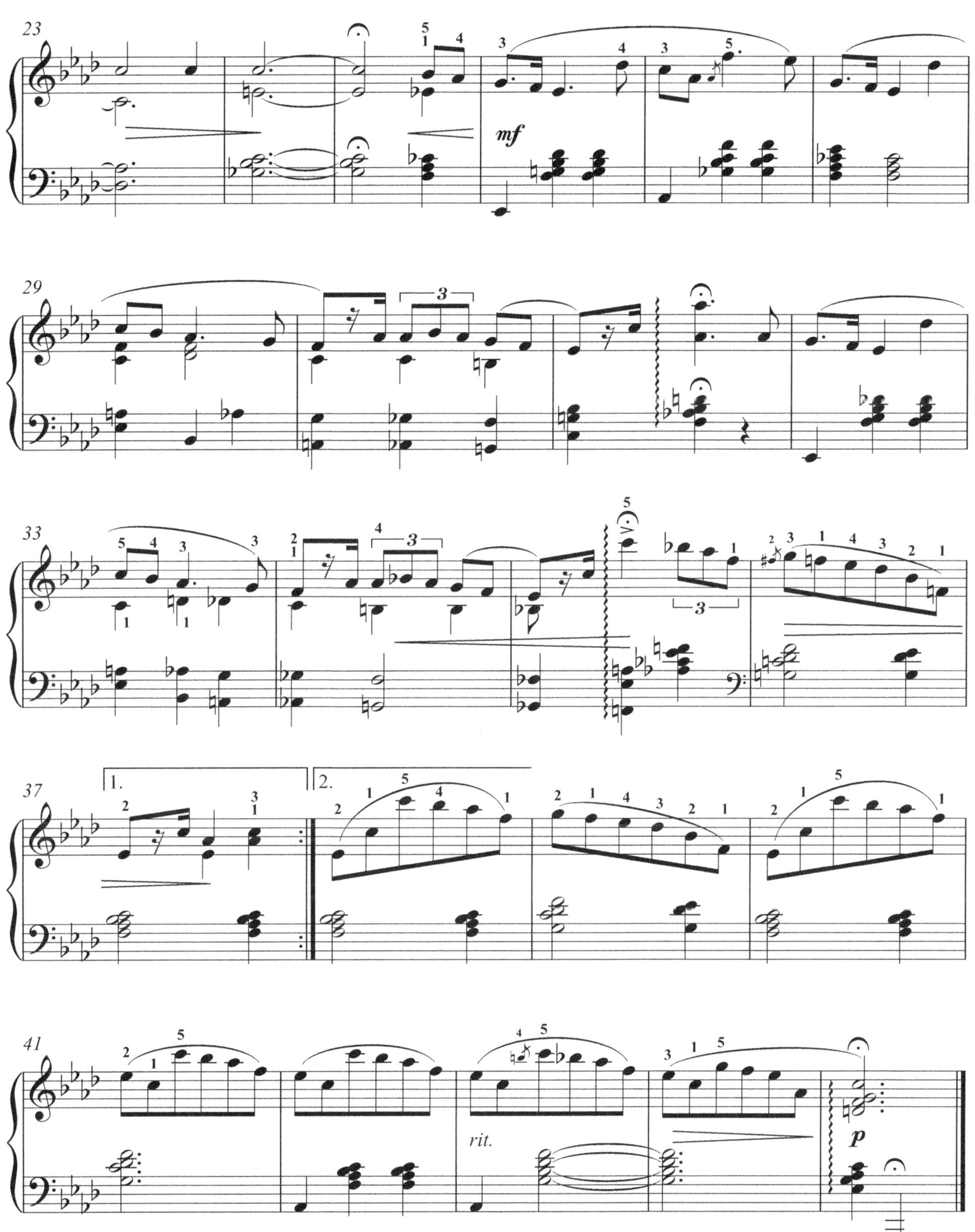
23
mf
29
33
37
1.
2.
41
rit.
p

Mazurka in A Minor

Op. 67, No. 4

Frédéric Chopin
Arranged by Bryce Russell

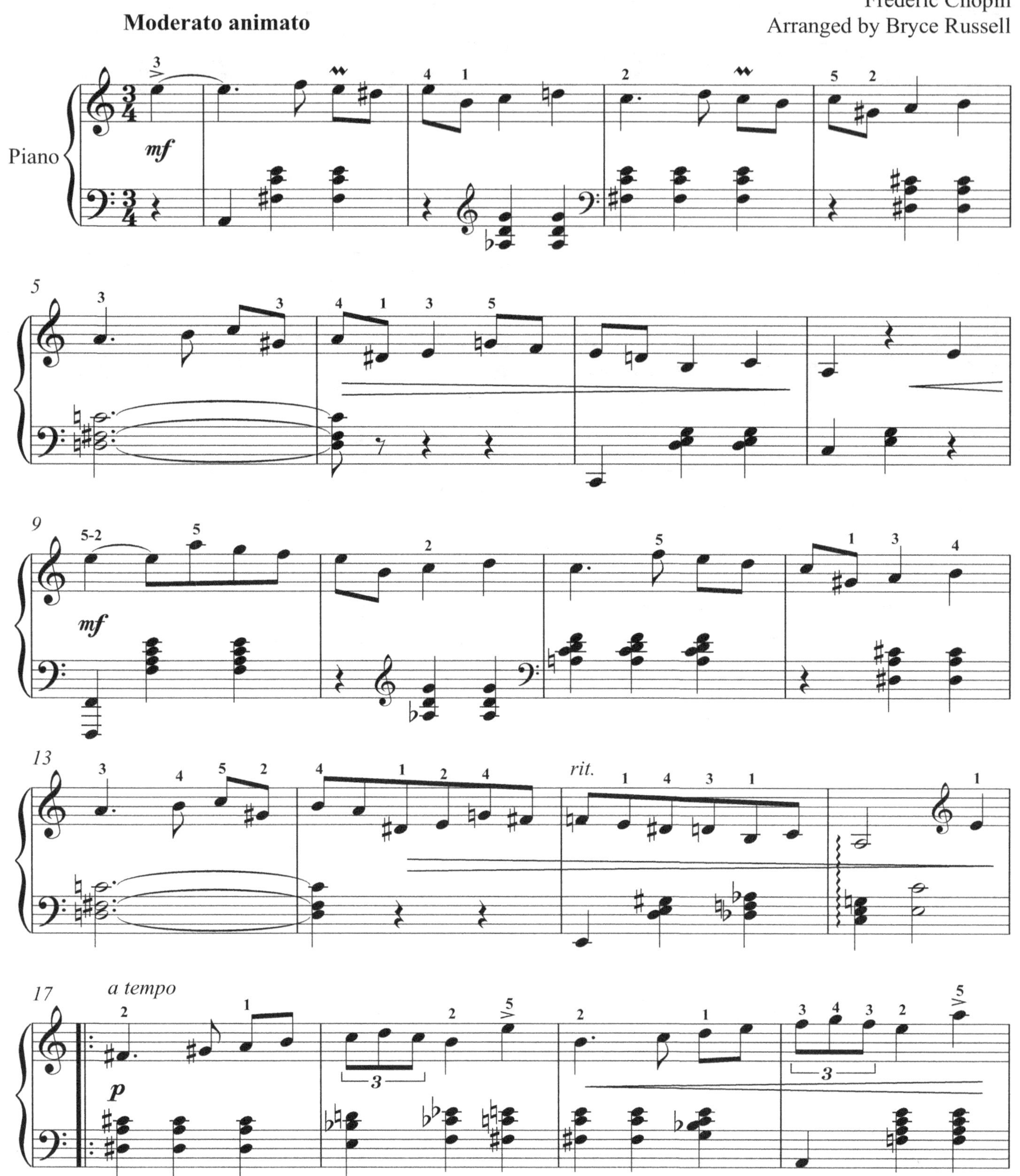

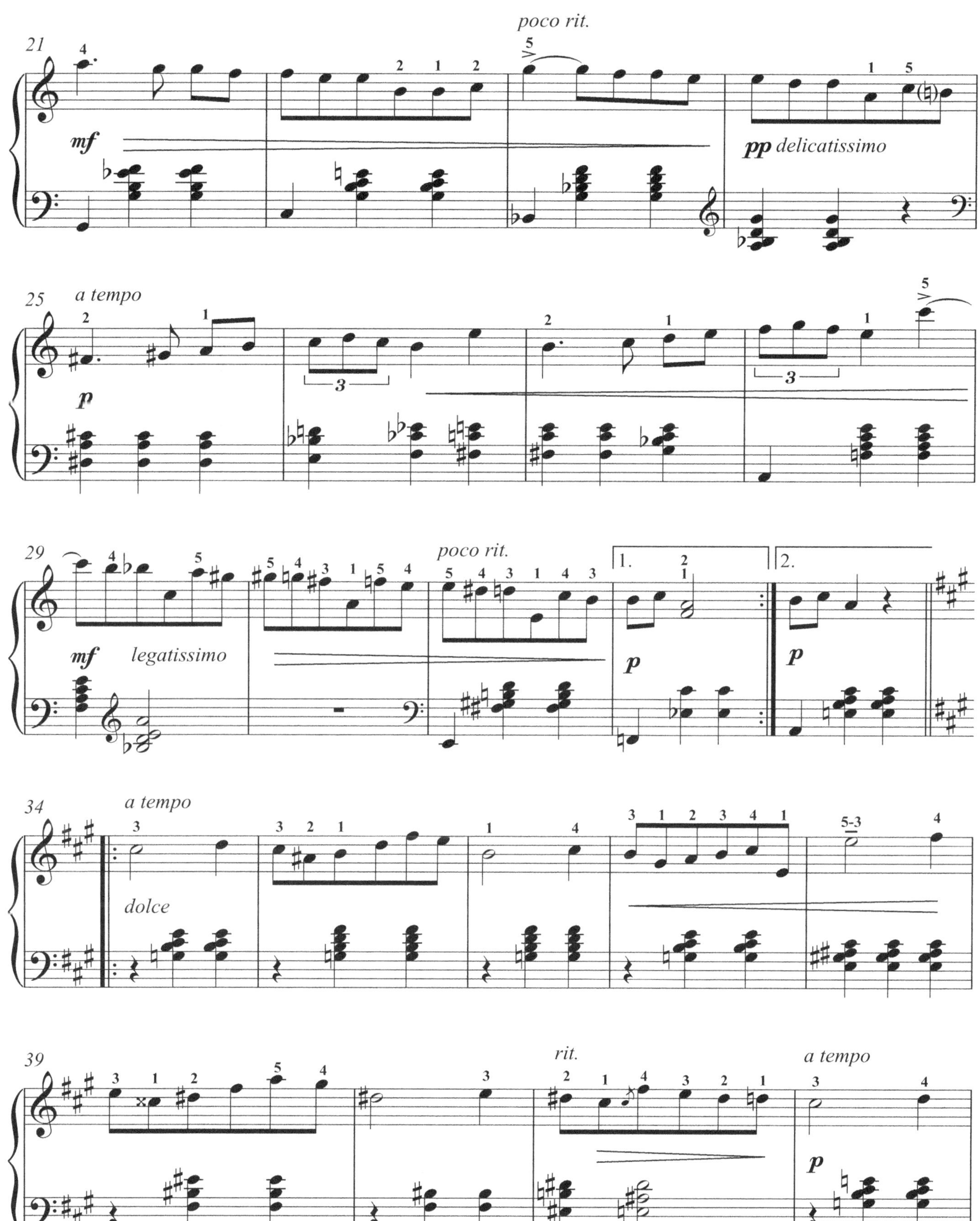
poco rit.
mf
pp delicatissimo
a tempo
p
mf
legatissimo
poco rit.
1.
2.
p
p
a tempo
dolce
rit.
a tempo
p

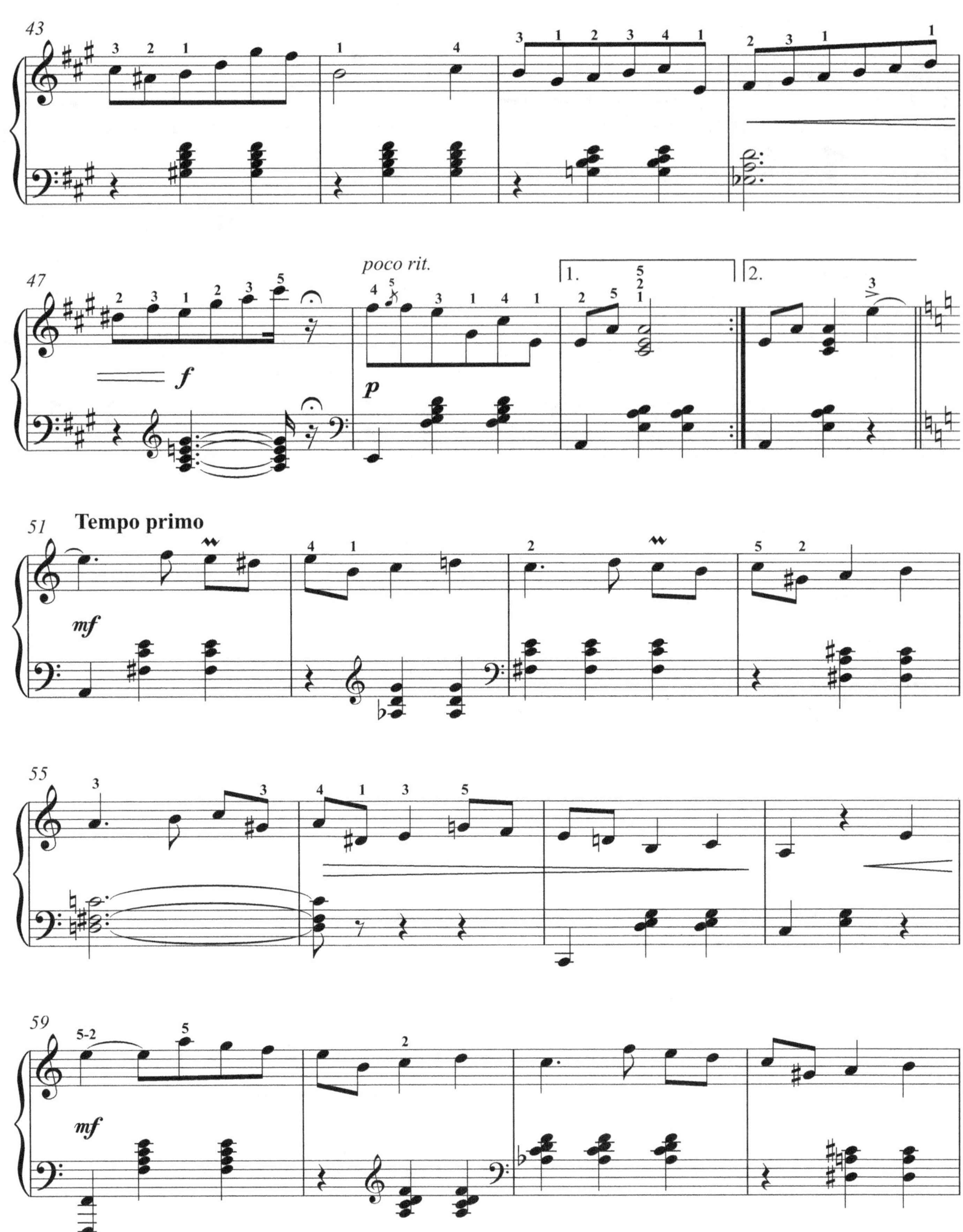
43
47
poco rit.
1.
2.
51
Tempo primo
55
59

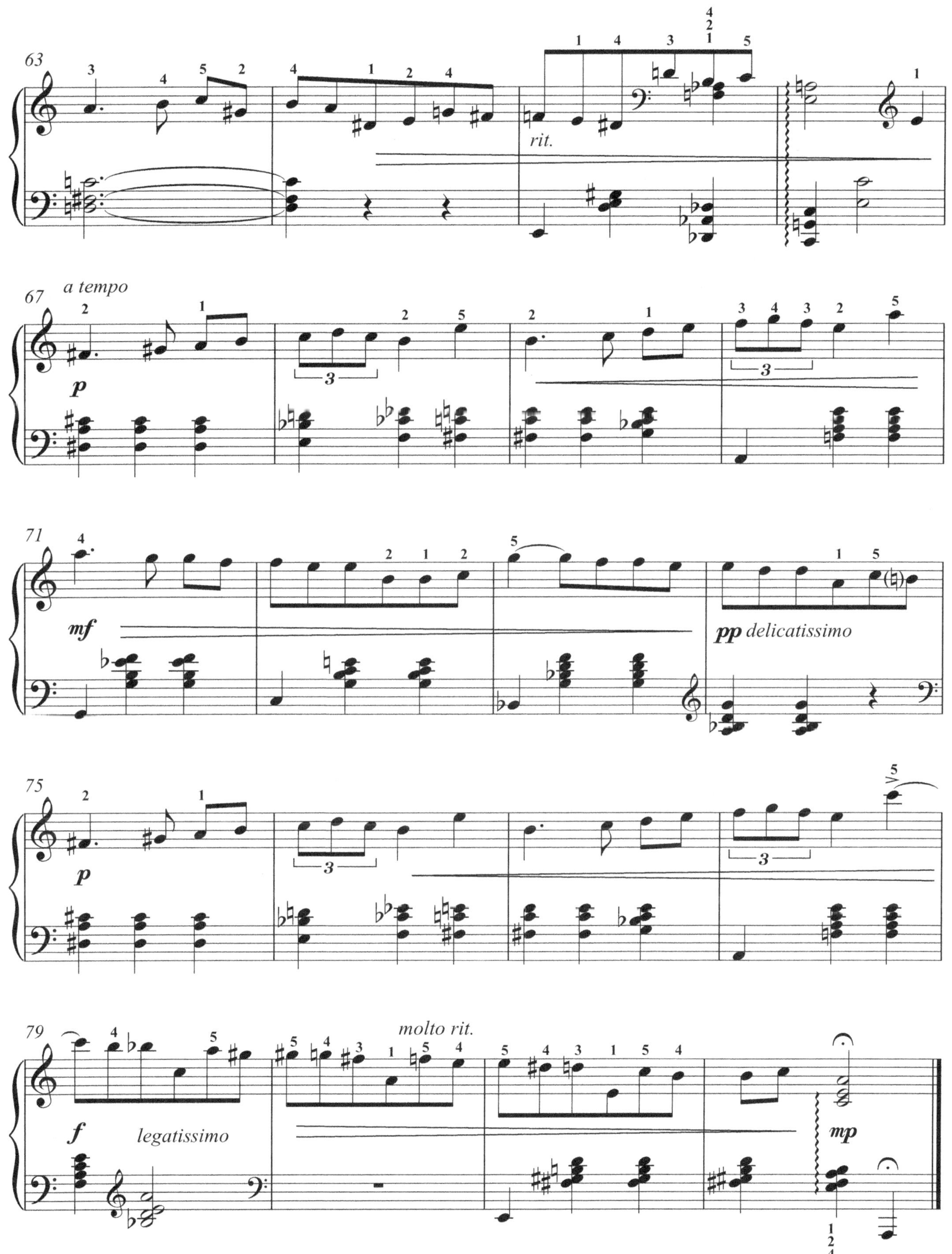
63
rit.
67
a tempo
p
71
mf
pp delicatissimo
75
p
79
f
legatissimo
molto rit.
mp

Mazurka in C Major

Op. 67, No. 3

Frédéric Chopin
Arranged by Bryce Russell

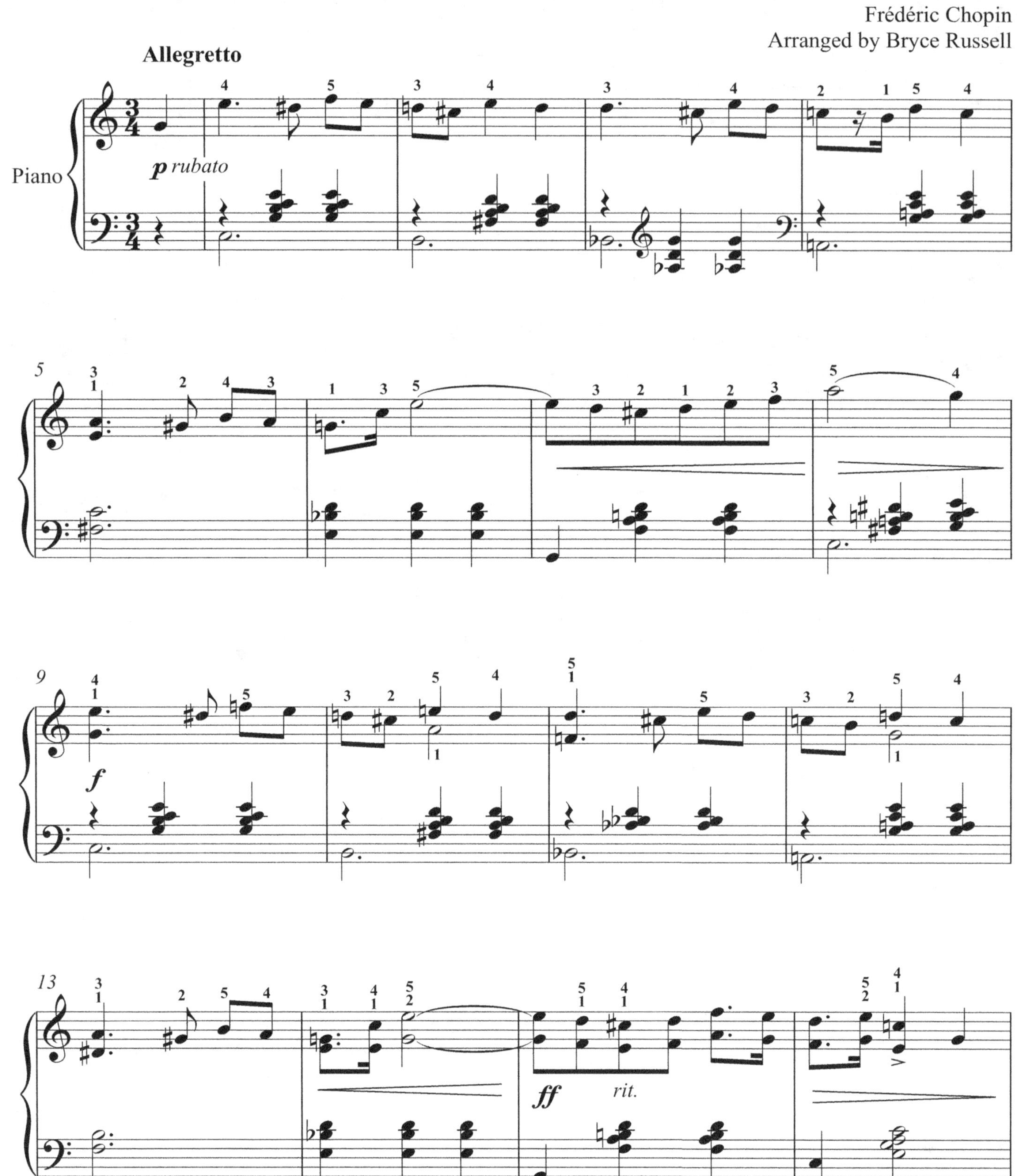

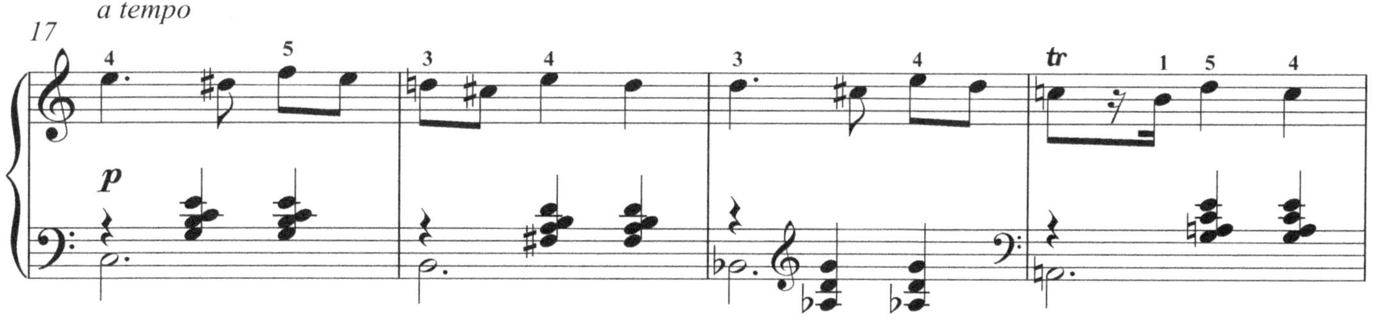
a tempo
17
p

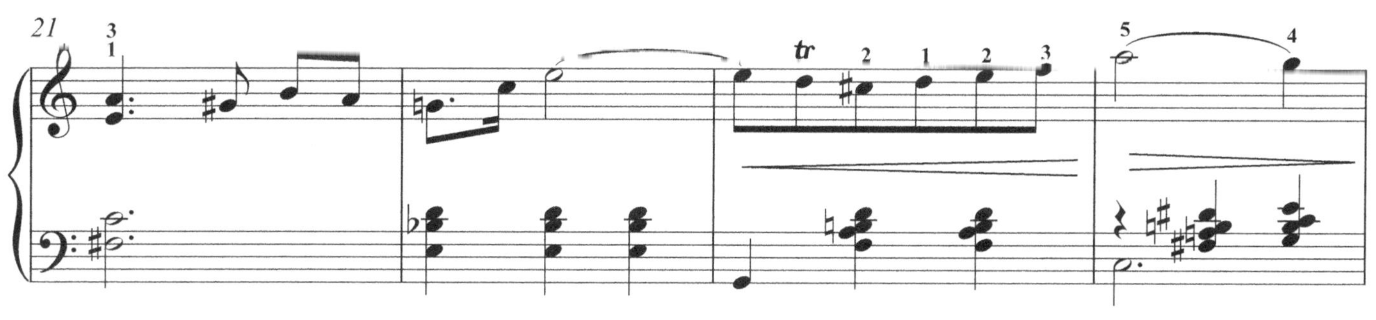
21

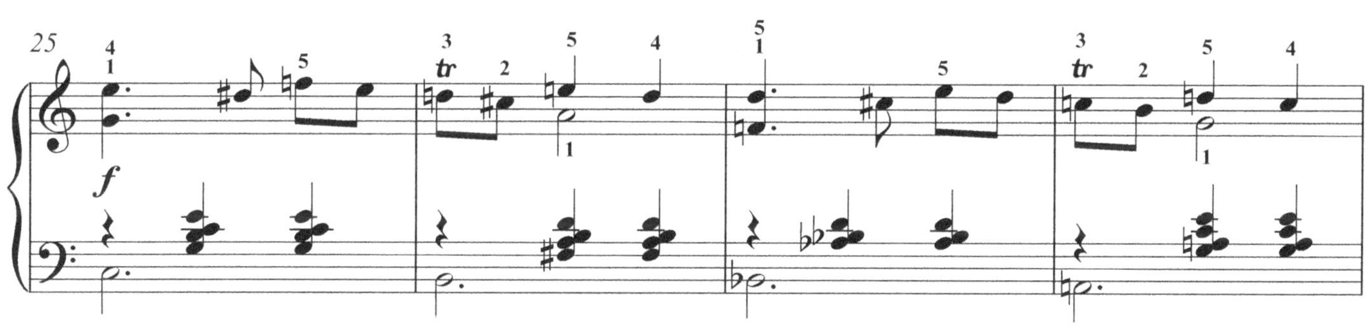
25
f

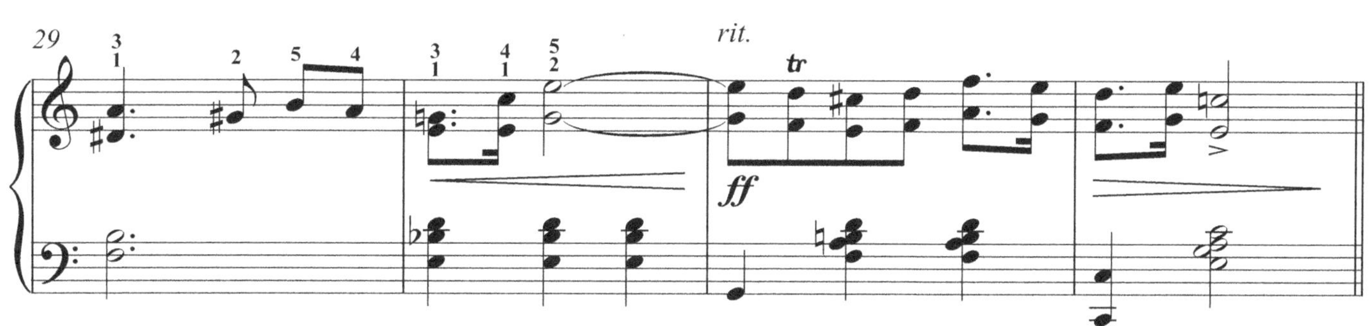
29
rit.
ff

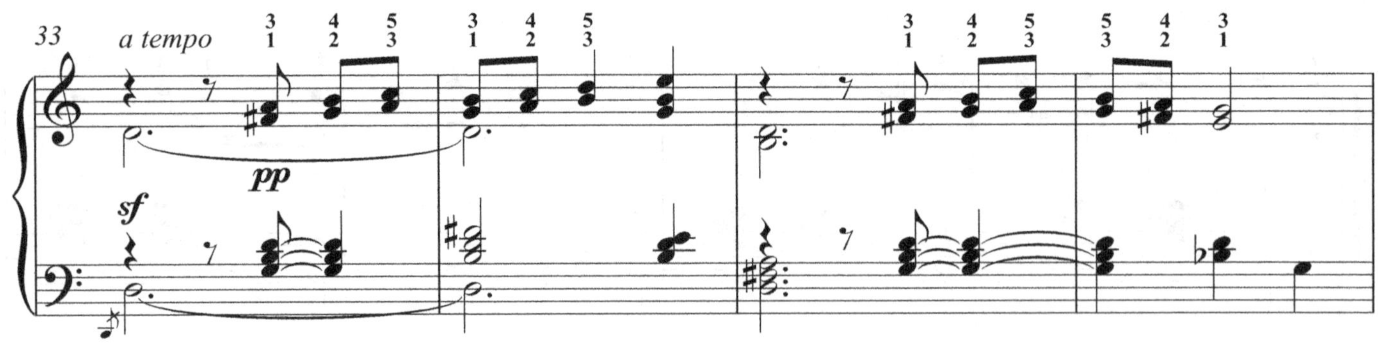
33
a tempo
pp
sf

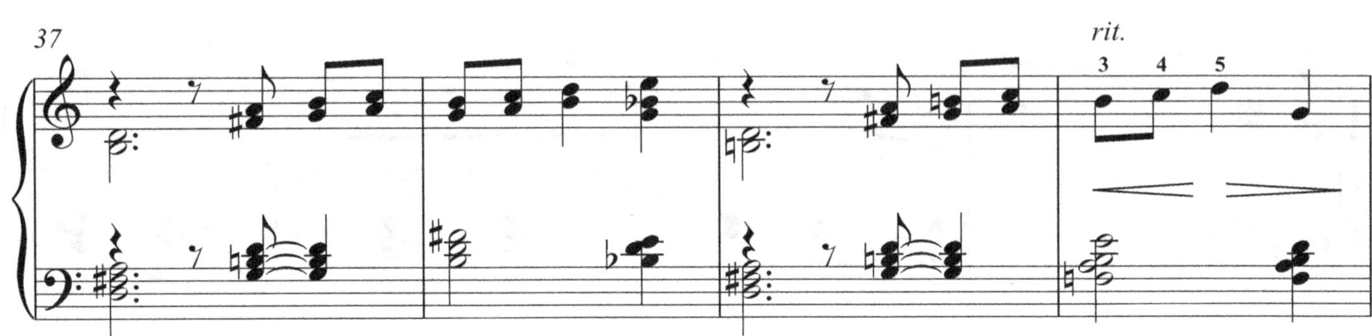
37
rit.

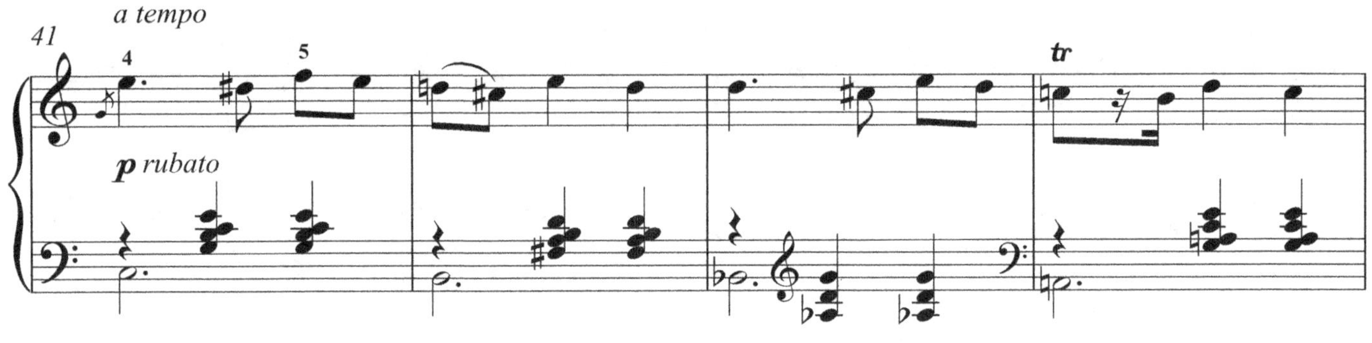
41
a tempo
p rubato
tr

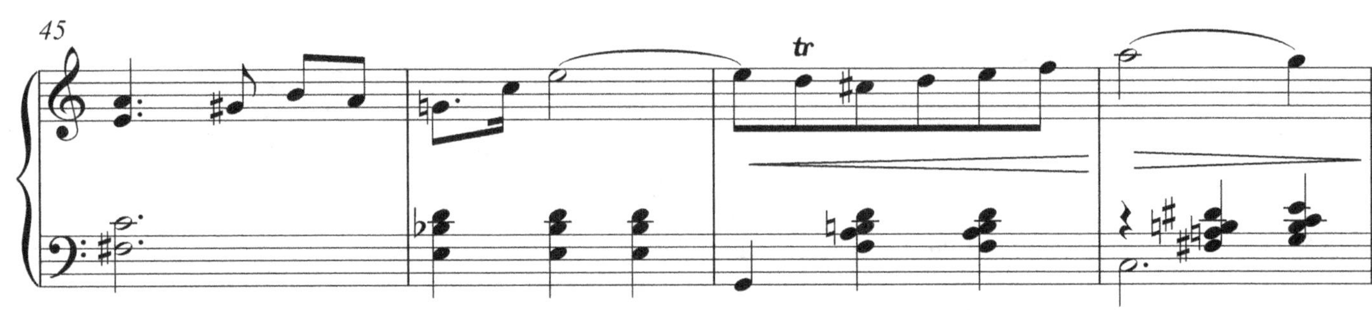
45
tr

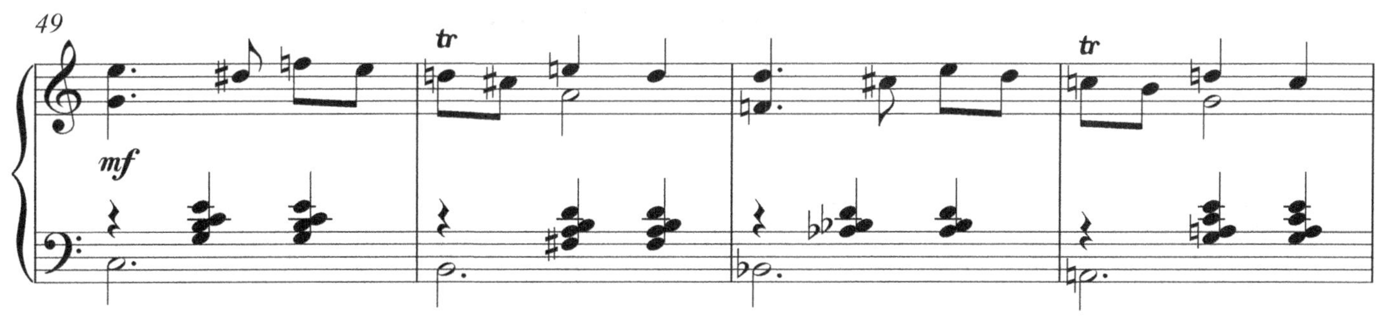
49
tr
mf
tr

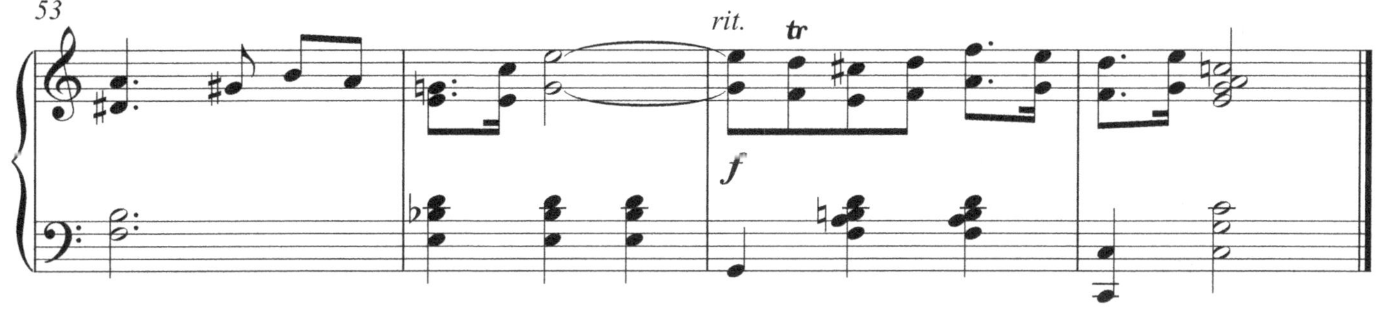
53
rit.
tr
f

Mazurka in F Major

Op. 68, No. 3

Frédéric Chopin

Arranged by Bryce Russell

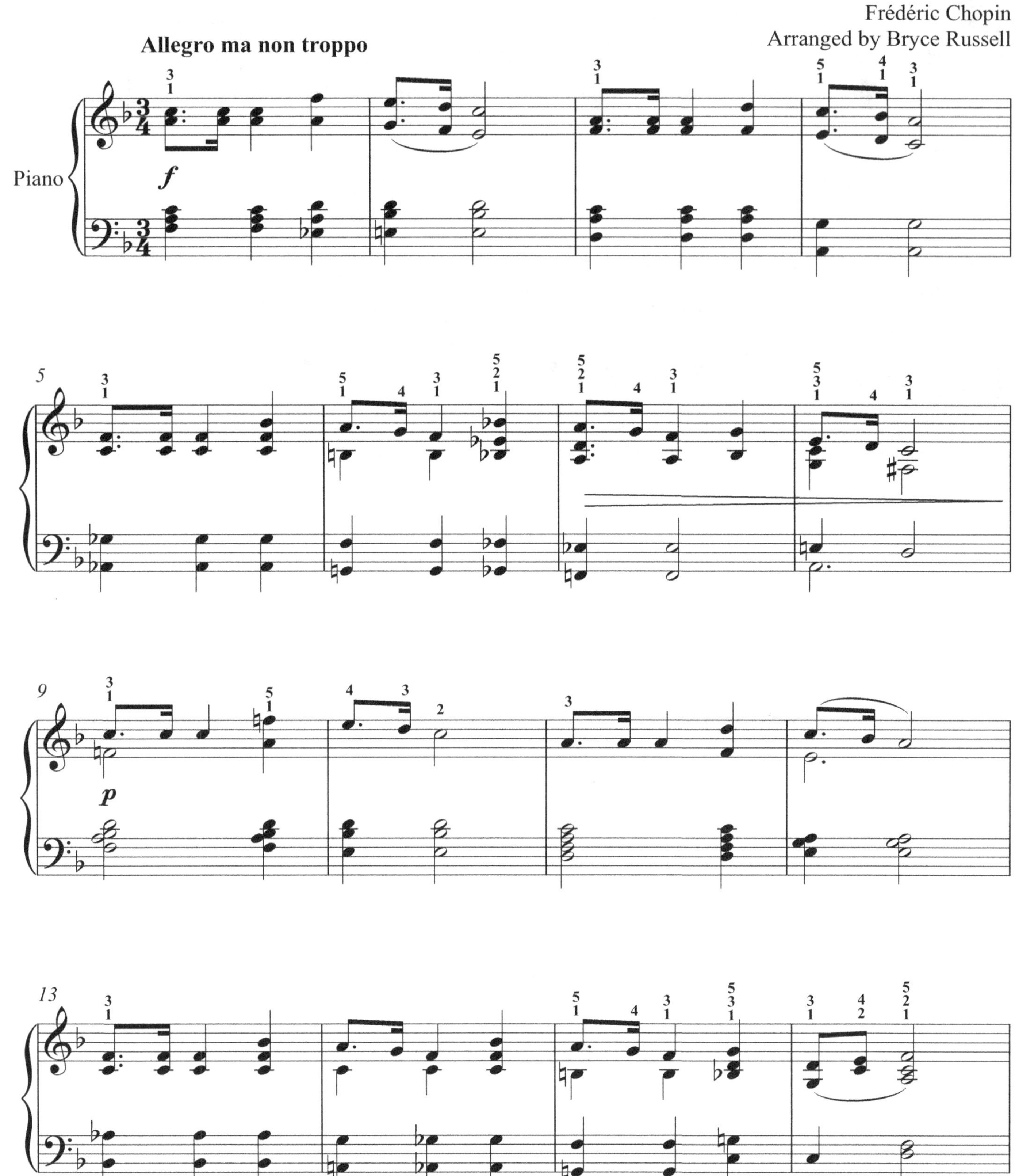

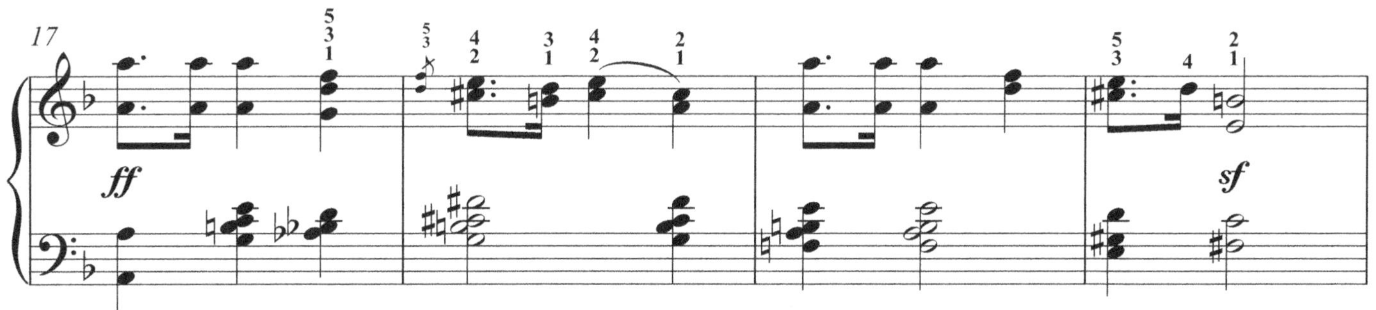
ff
sf
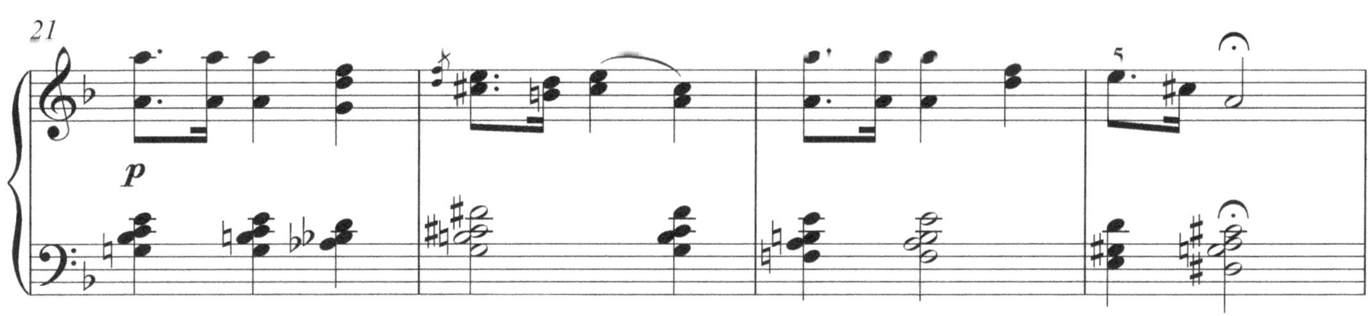
p
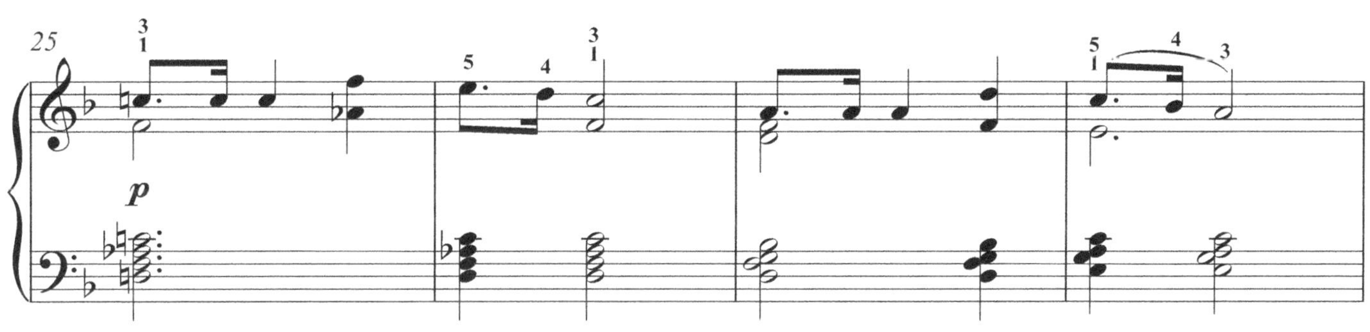
p
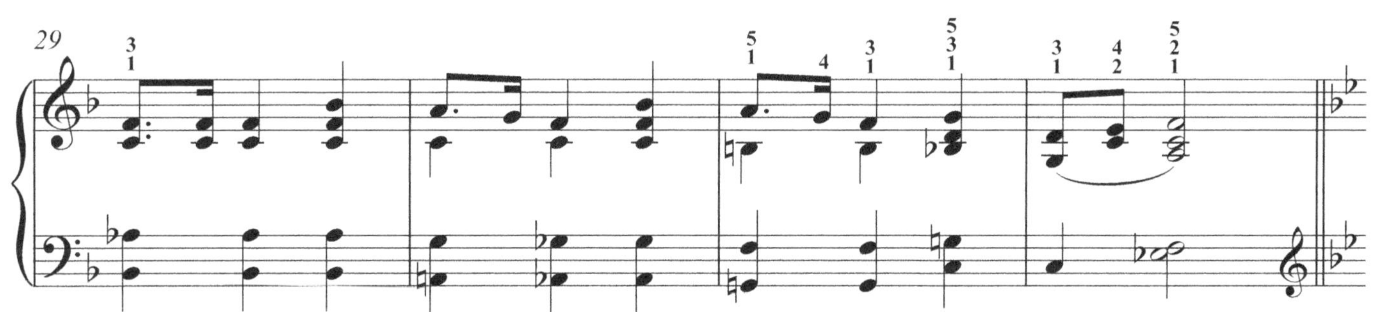

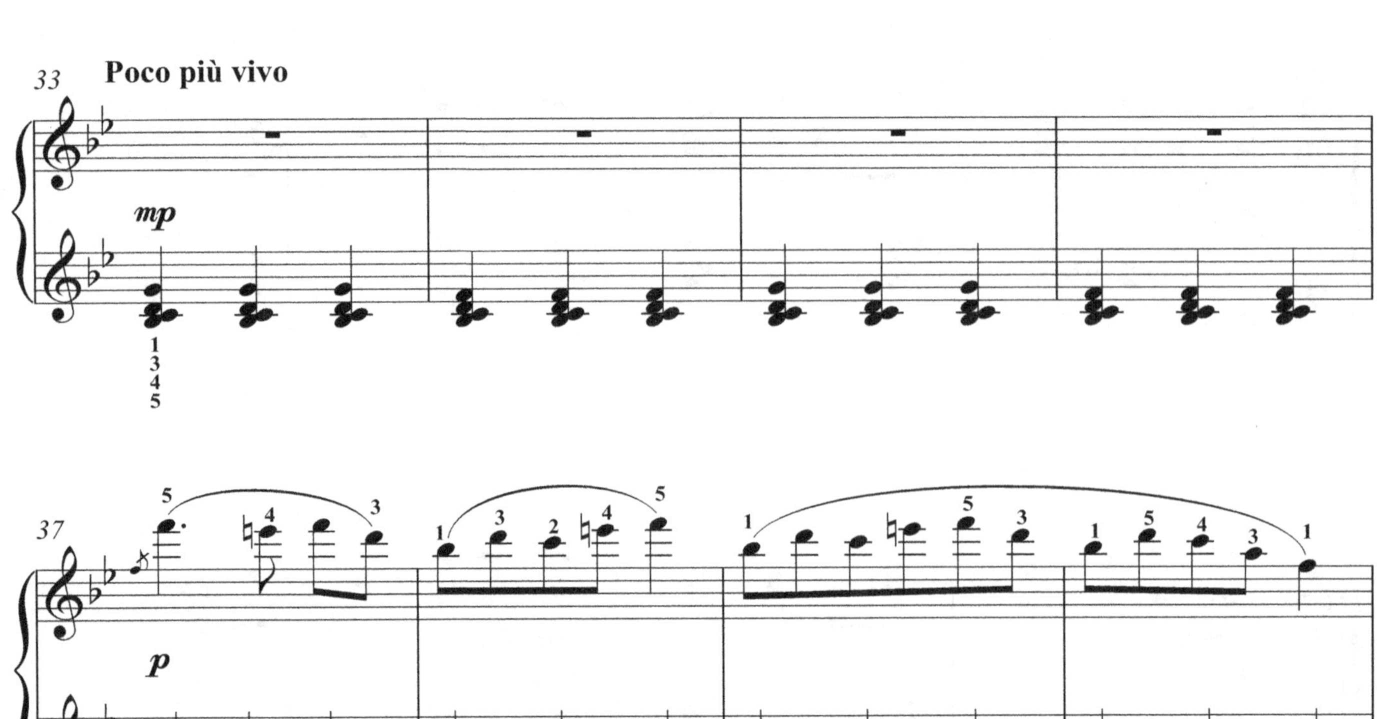
33
Poco più vivo
mp
1
3
4
5
37
5
4
3
1
3
2
4
5
1
5
3
1
5
4
3
1
p

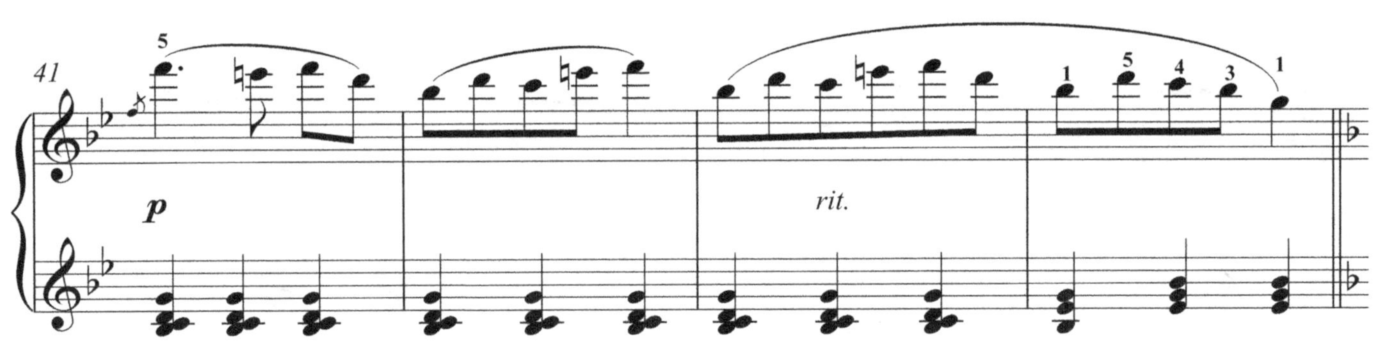
41
5
1
5
4
3
1
p
rit.

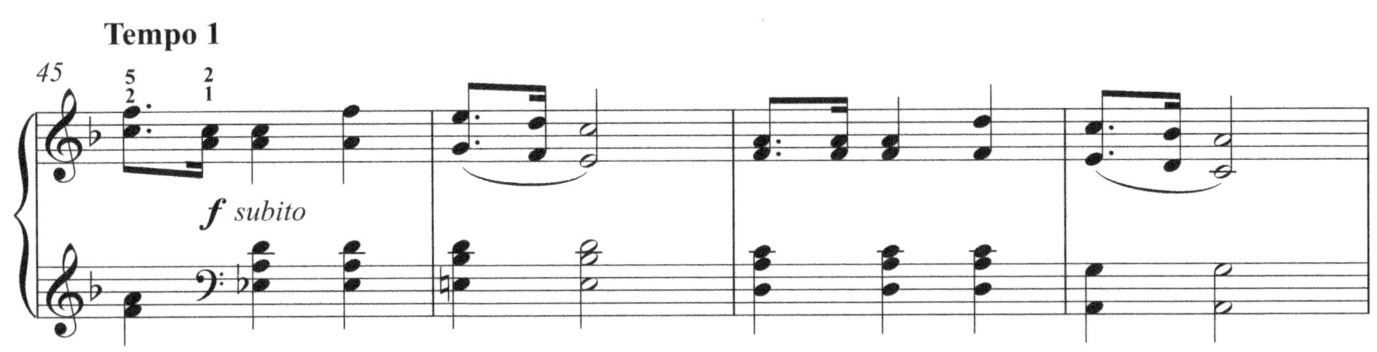
Tempo 1
45
5
2
2
1
f subito

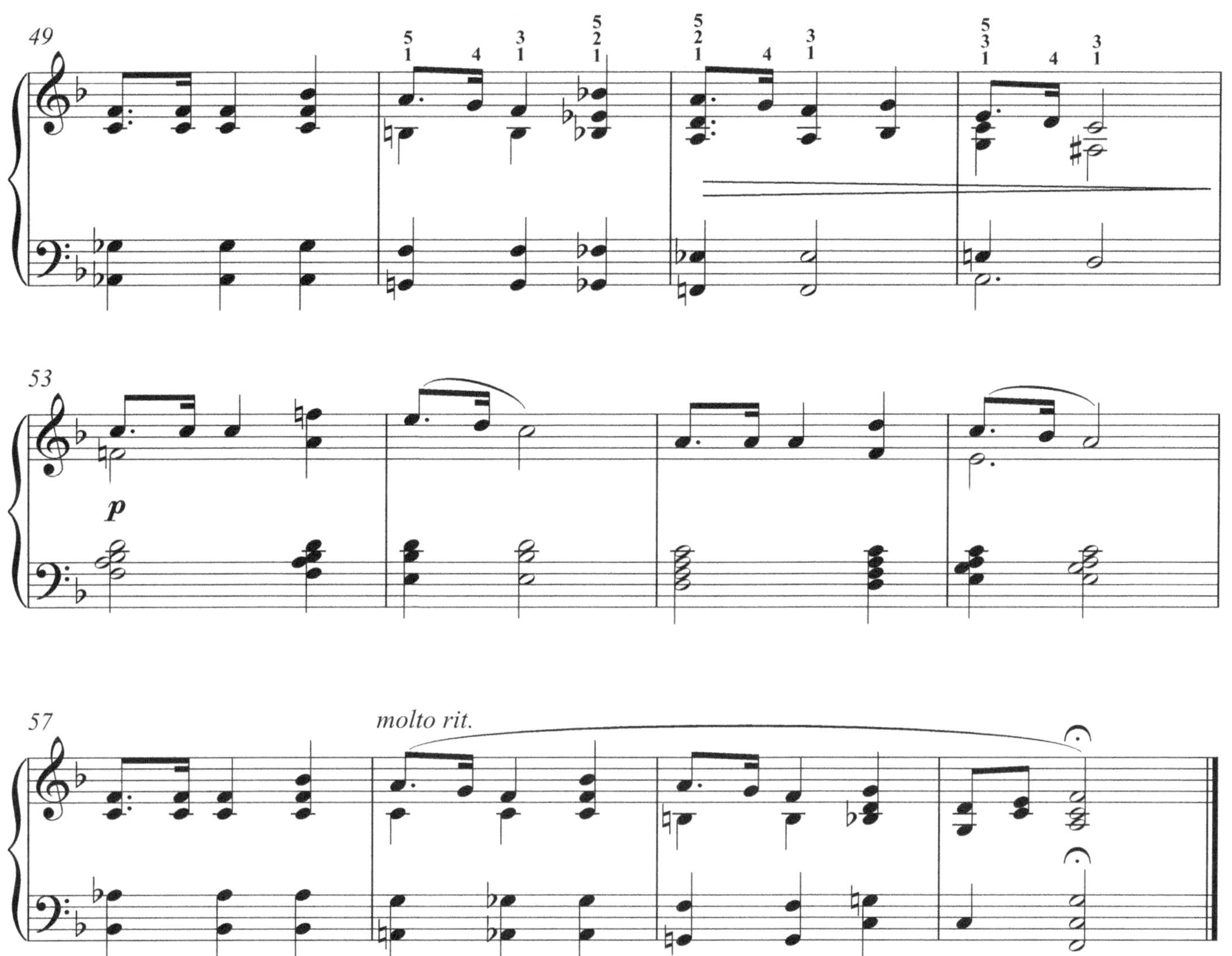
49
5
1
4
3
1
5
2
1
5
2
1
4
3
1
5
3
1
4
3
1
53
p
57
molto rit.

Mazurka in G Minor

Op. 67, No. 2

Frédéric Chopin
Arranged by Bryce Russell

Cantabile

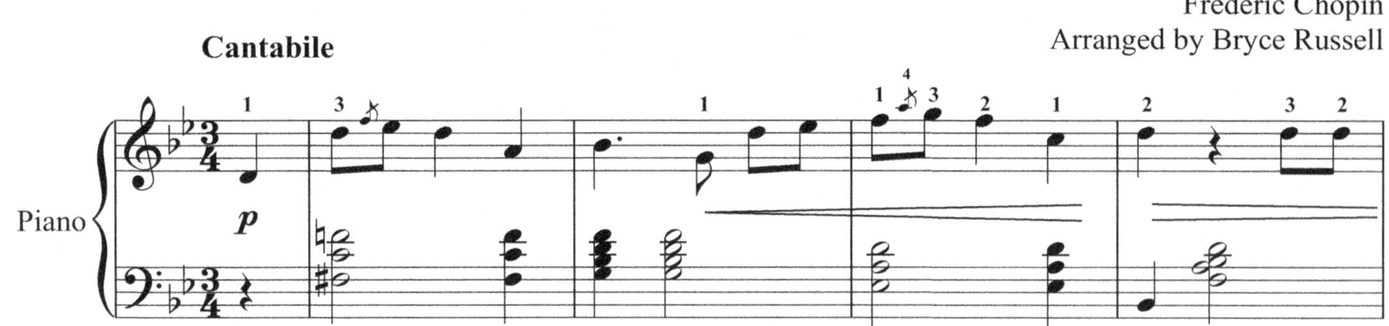

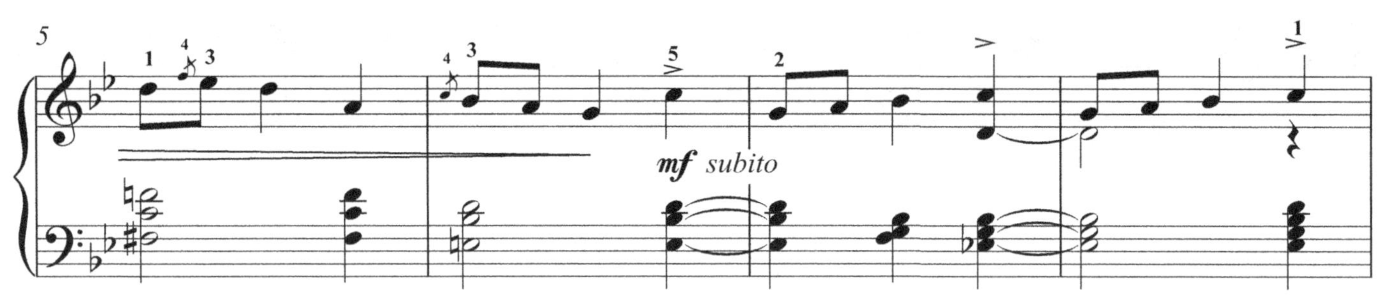

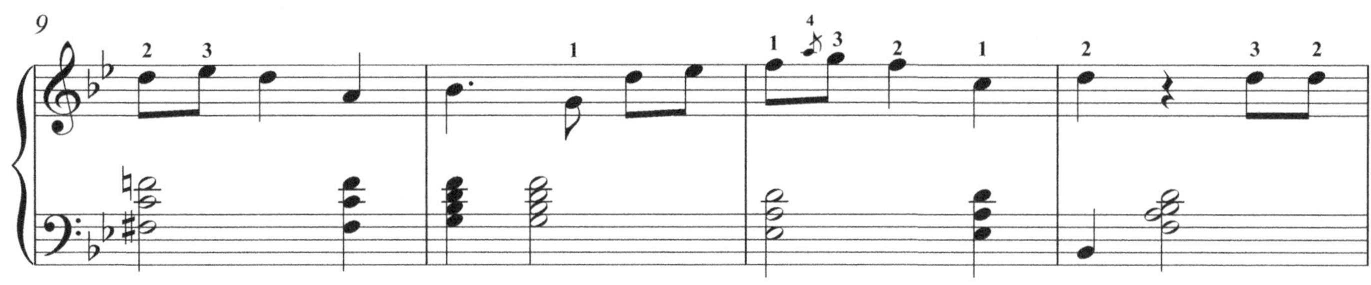

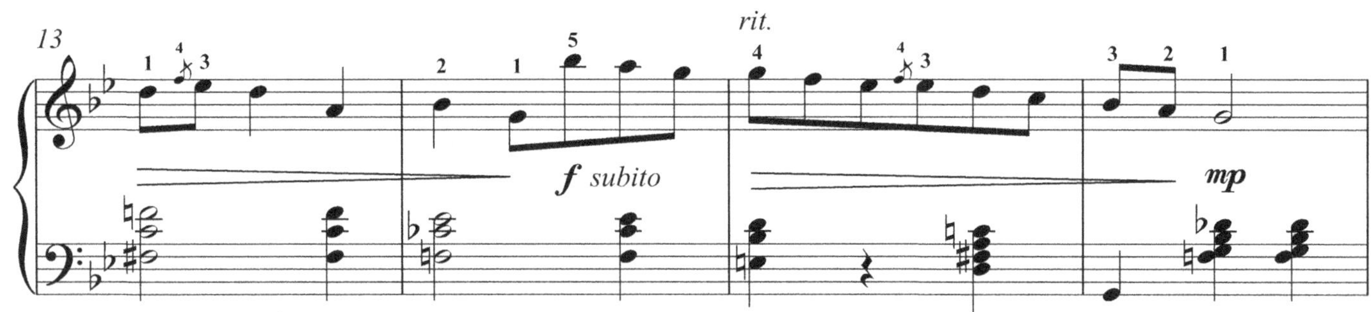

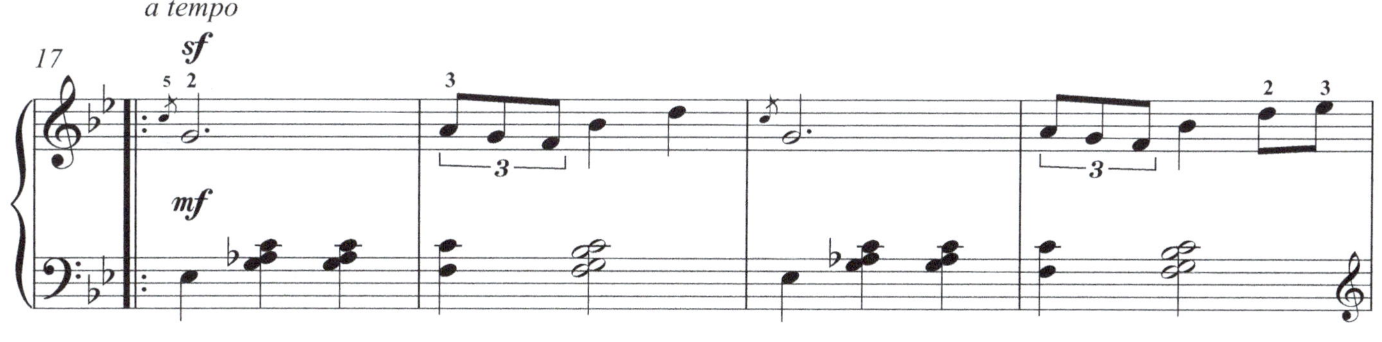
a tempo
17
sf
mf
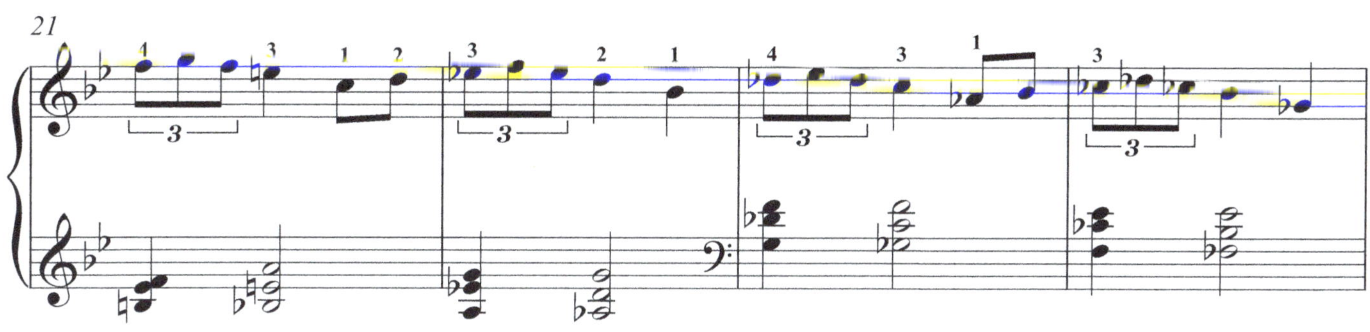
21
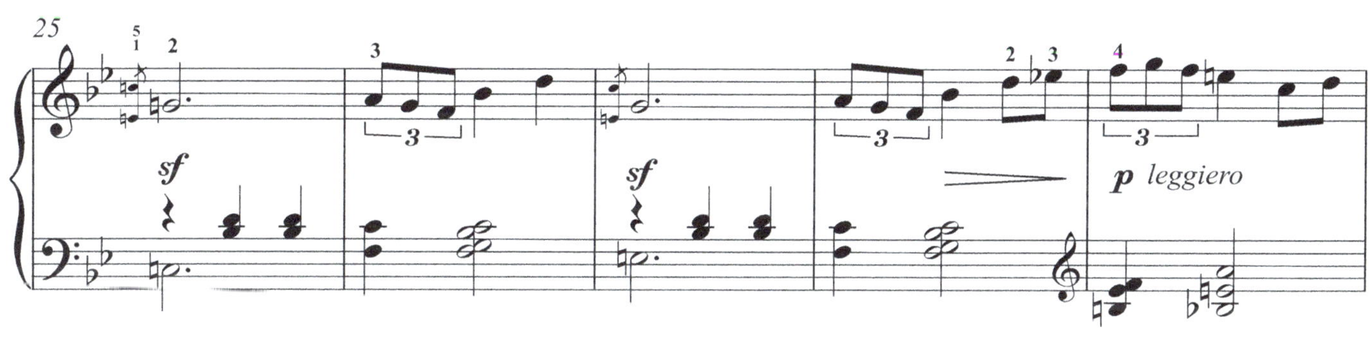
25
sf
sf
p leggiero
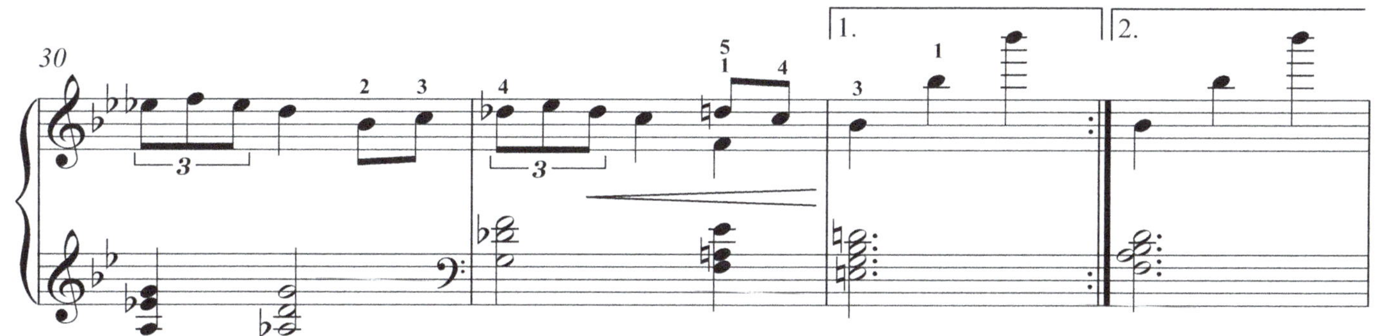
30
1.
2.

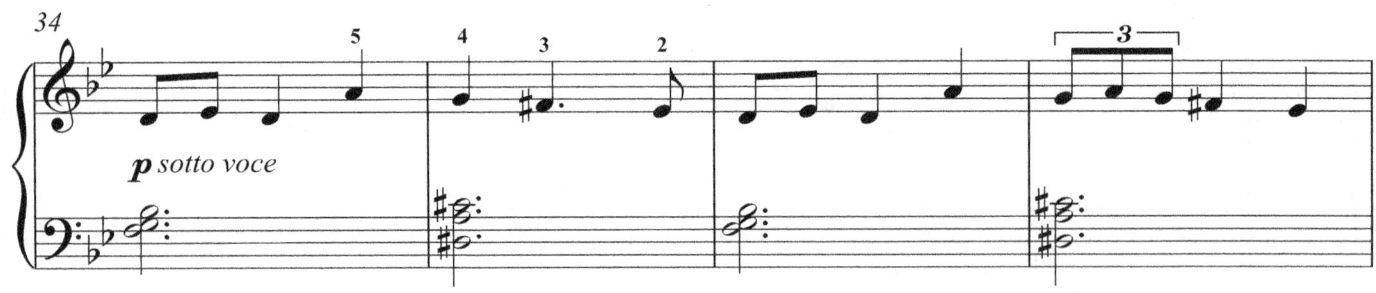
34
p sotto voce
5
4
3
2
3

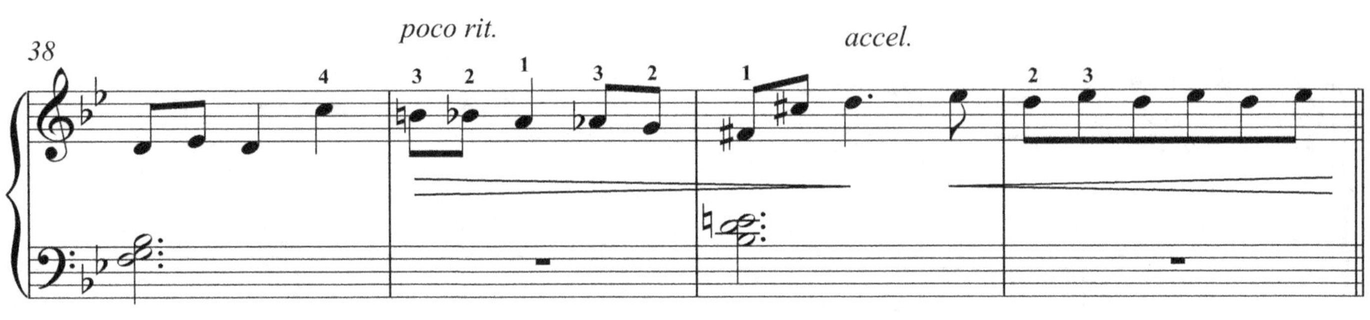
38
poco rit.
accel.
4
3
2
1
3
2
1
2
3

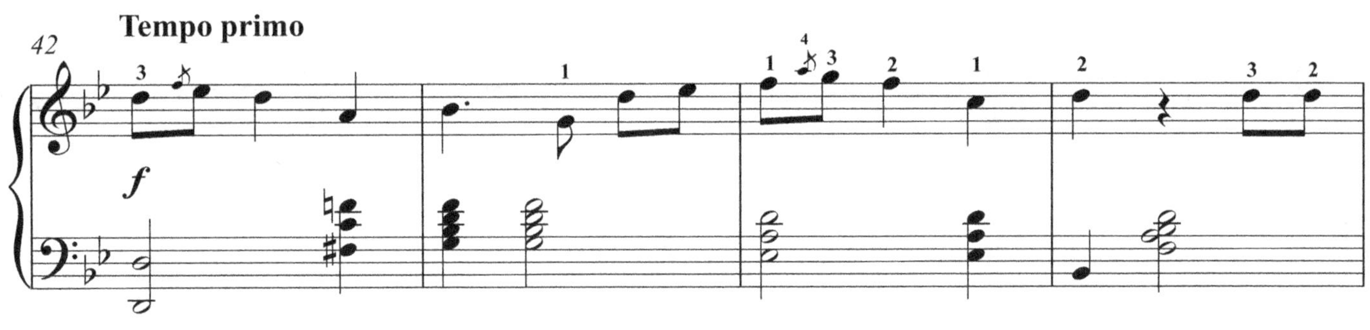
42
Tempo primo
f

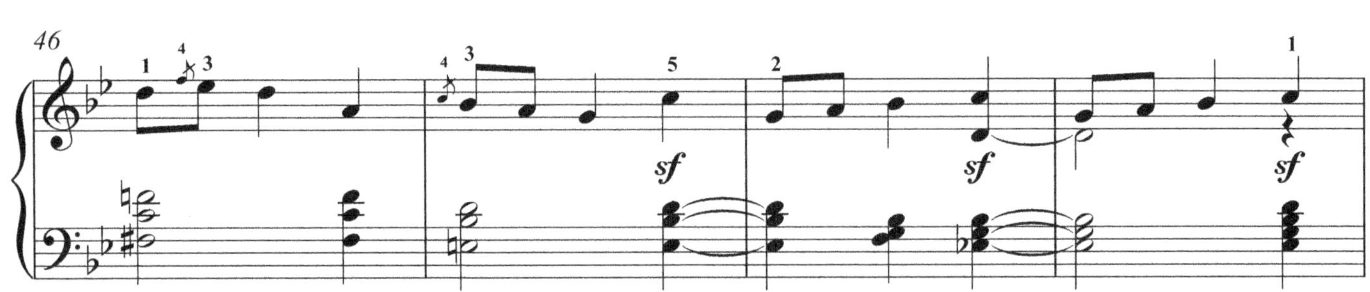
46
sf
sf
sf

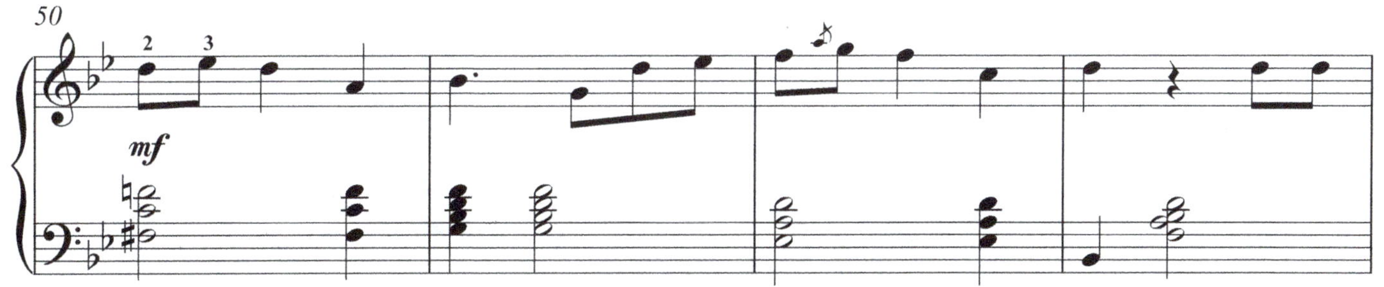
50
mf

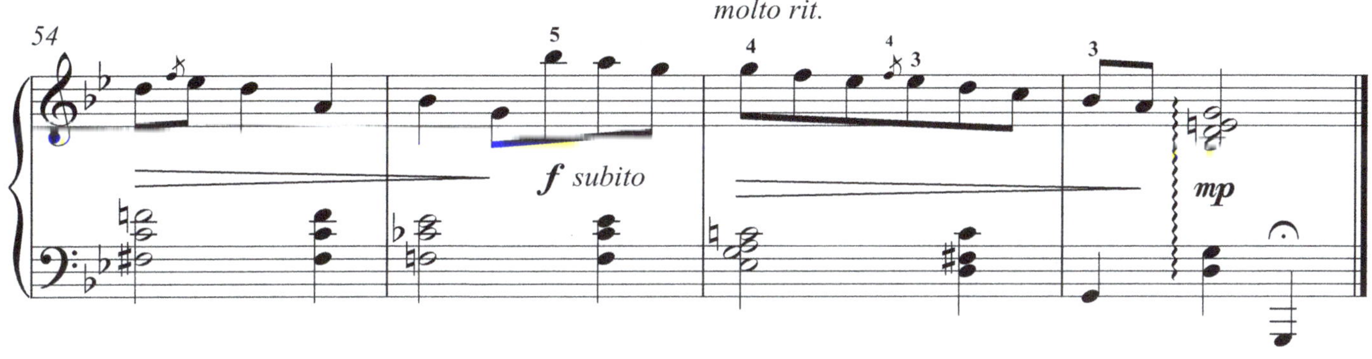
54
molto rit.
f subito
mp

Mazurka in G♯ Minor

Op. 33, No. 1

Frédéric Chopin
Arranged by Bryce Russell

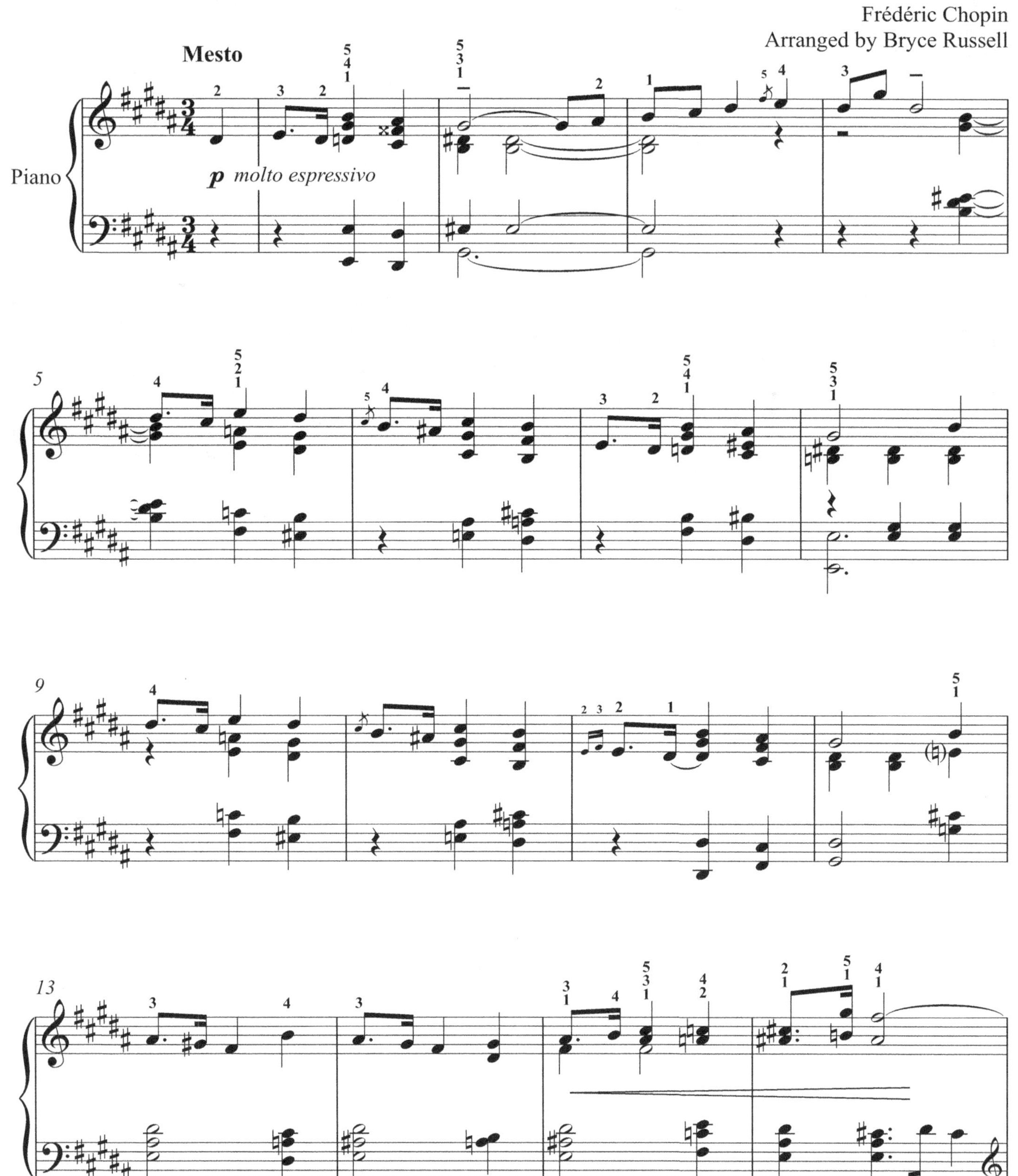

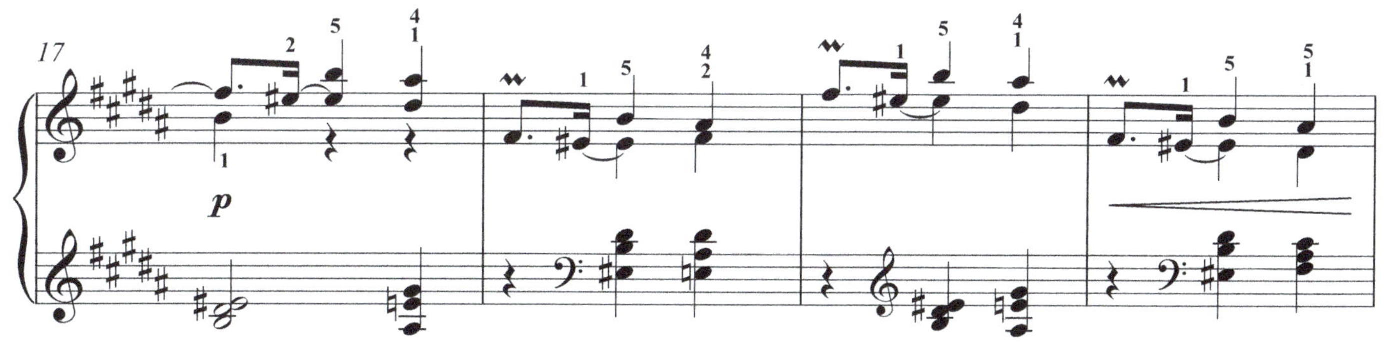
17
p
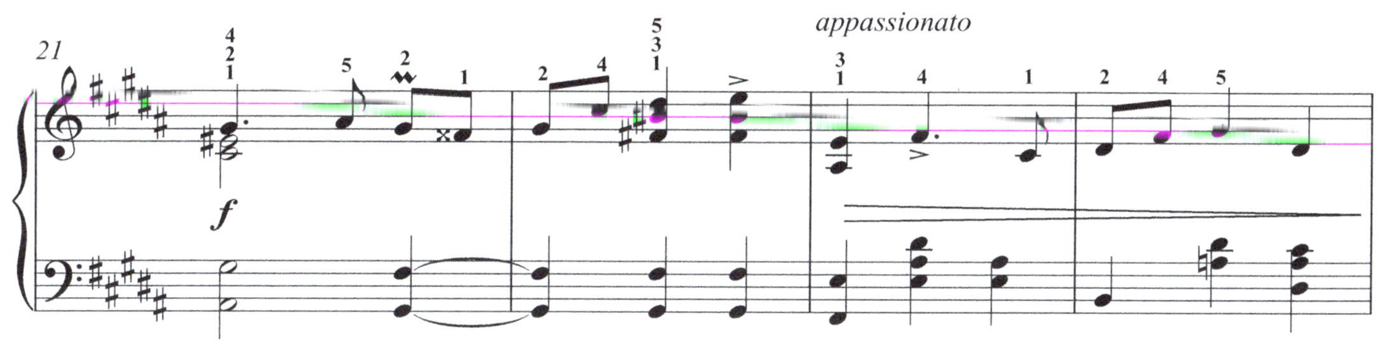
21
appassionato
f
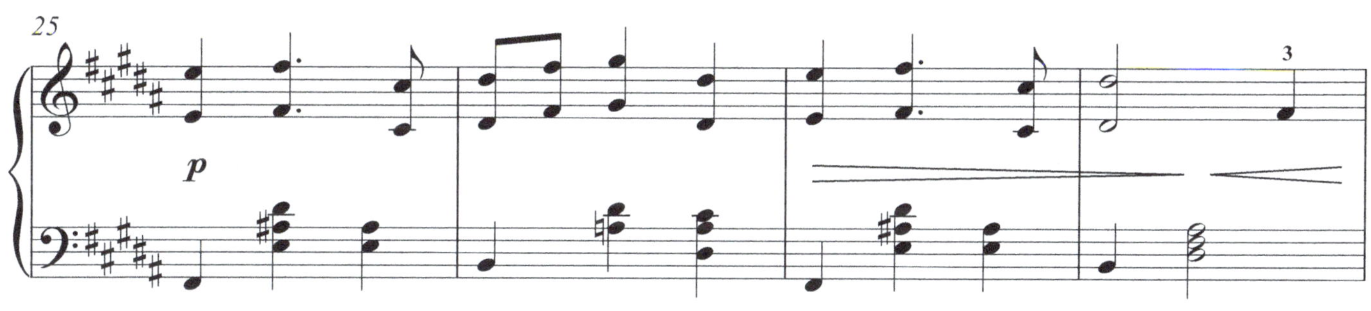
25
p
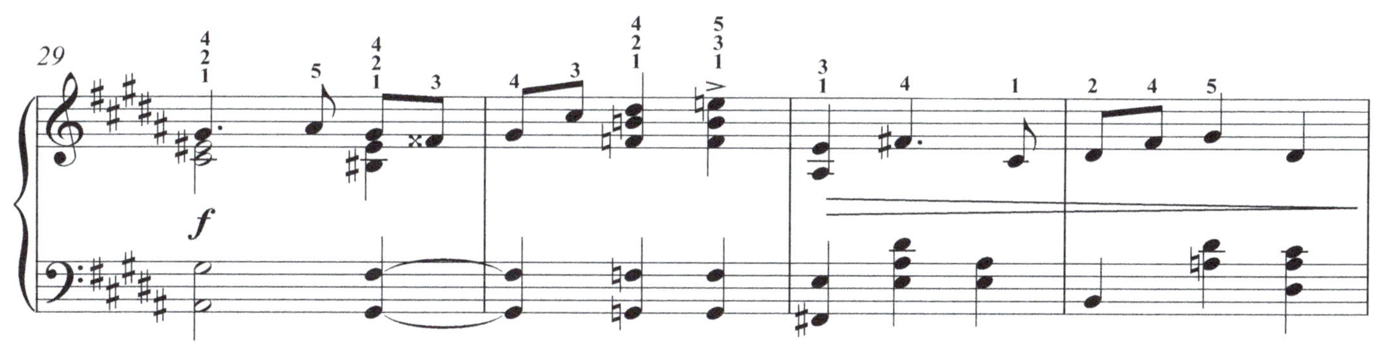
29
f

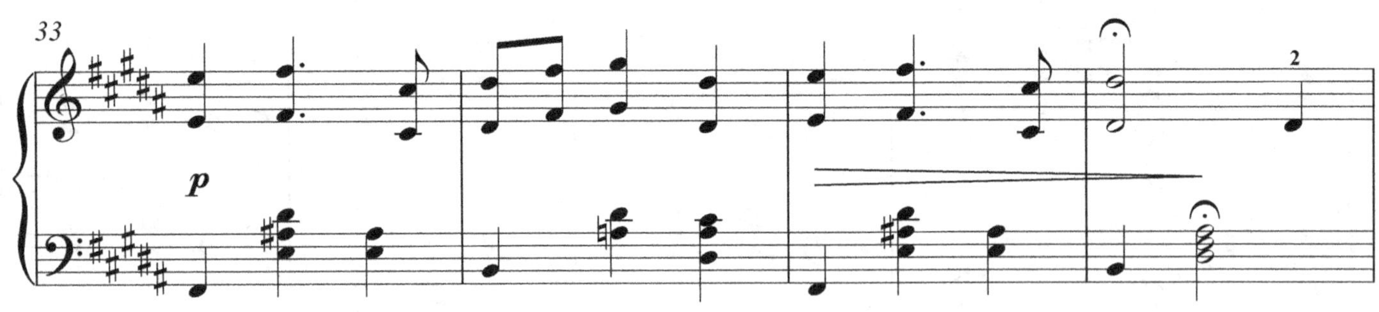
33
p
2

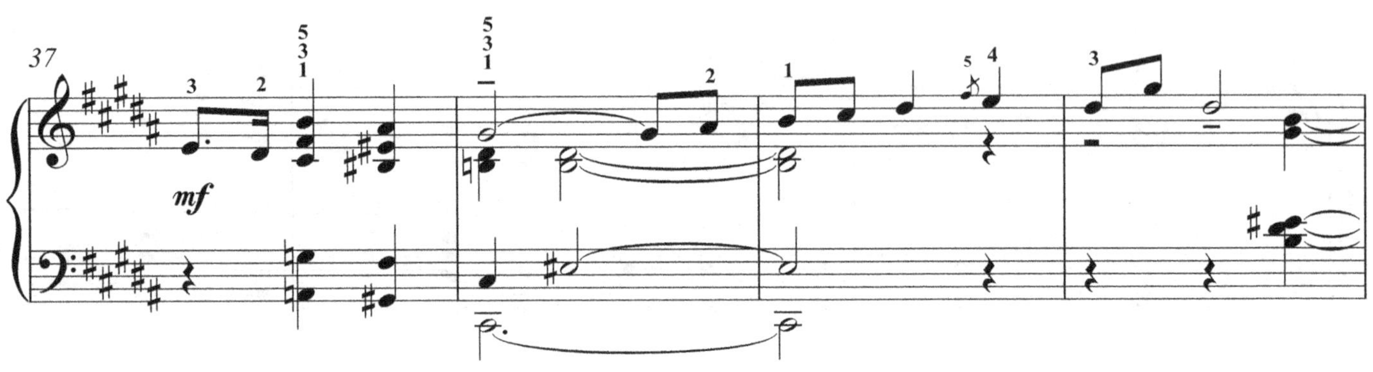
37
3
2
5
3
1
mf
5
3
1
2
1
5
4
3

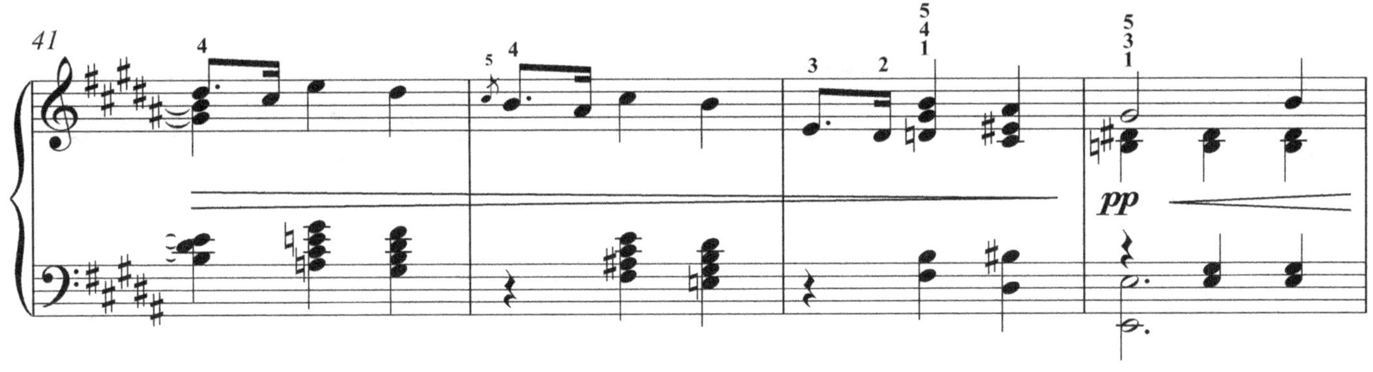
41
4
5
4
3
2
5
4
1
5
3
1
pp

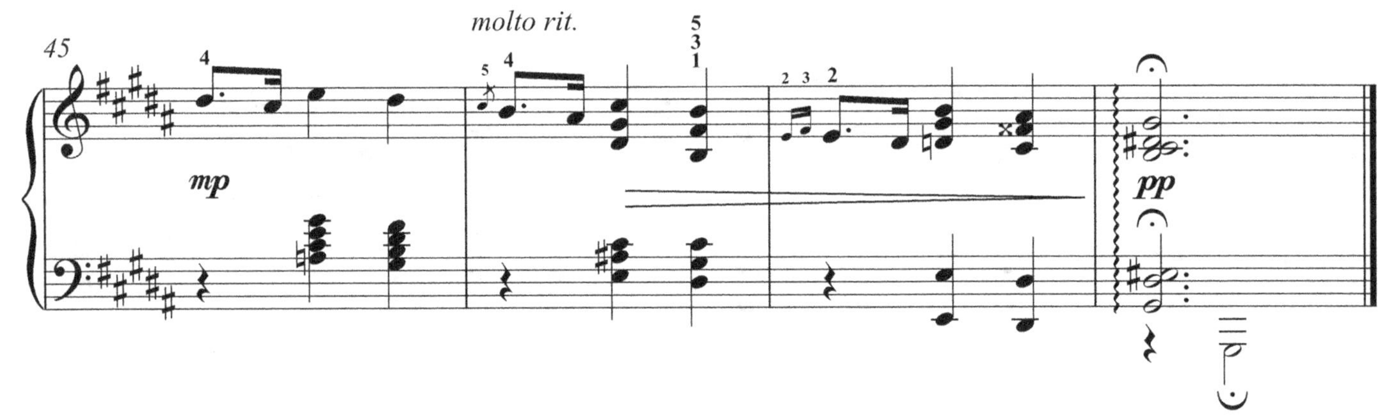
45
molto rit.
4
mp
5
4
5
3
1
2
3
2
pp

Prelude in A Major

Op. 28, No. 7

Frédéric Chopin
Arranged by Bryce Russell

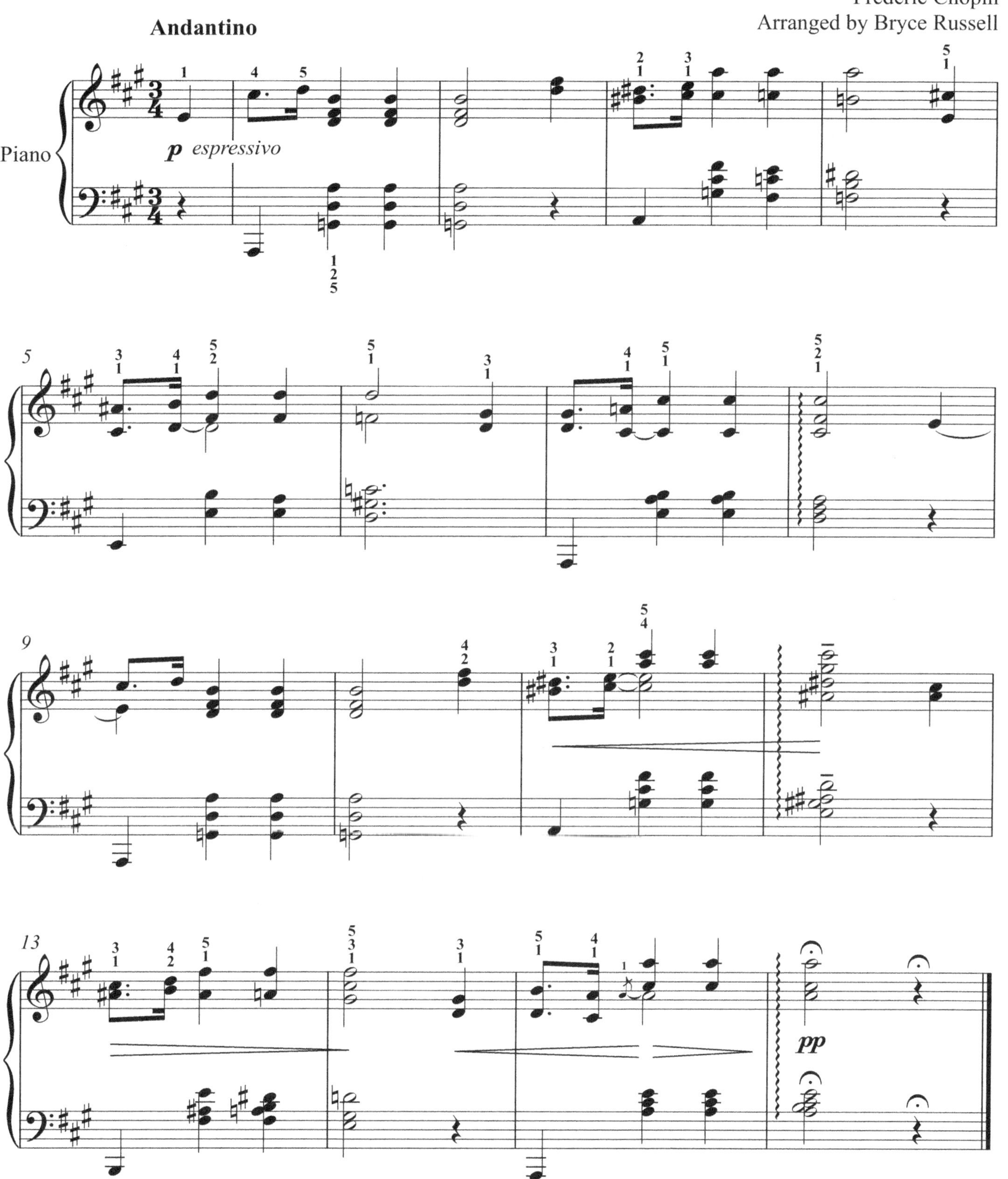

Prelude in E Minor

Op. 28, No. 4

Frédéric Chopin
Arranged by Bryce Russell

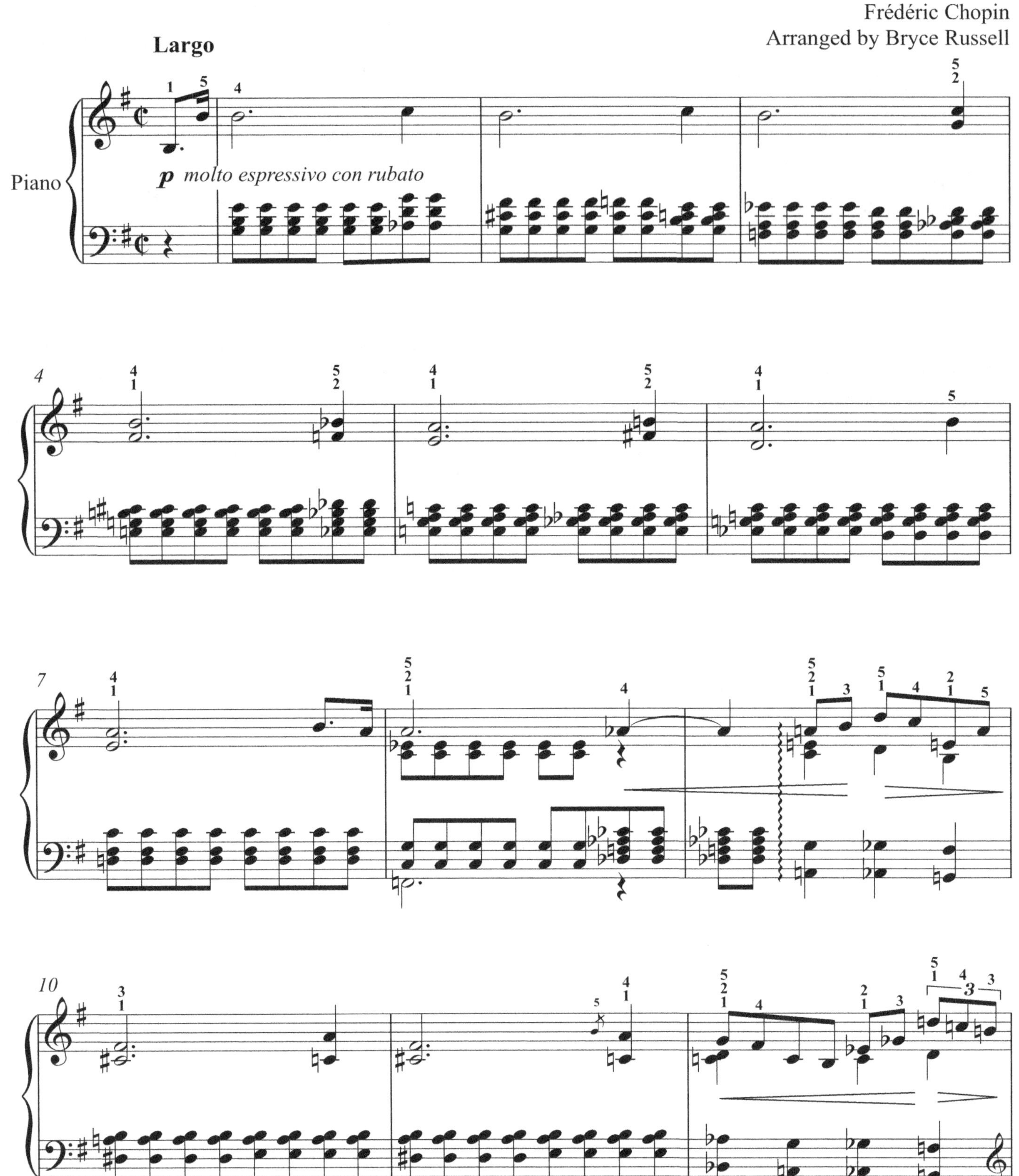

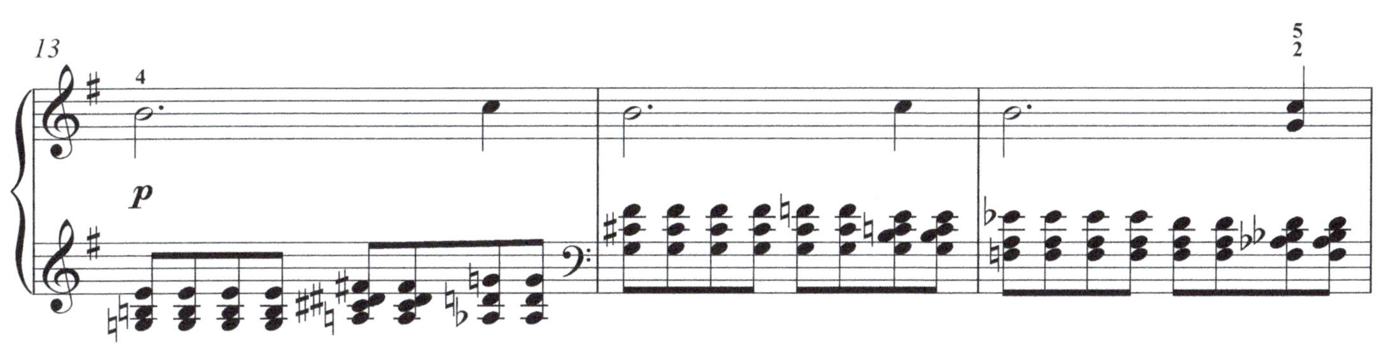
13
p

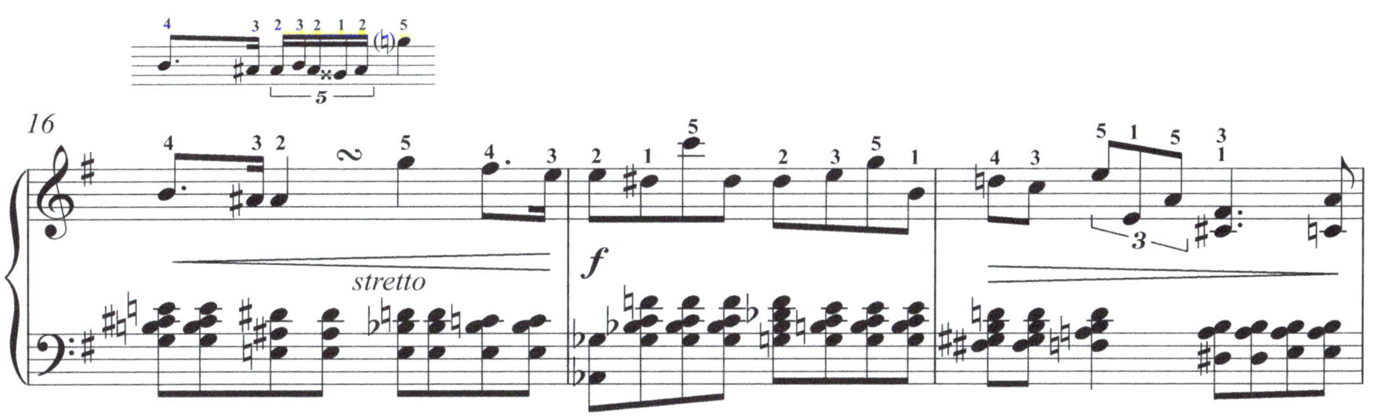
16
stretto
f

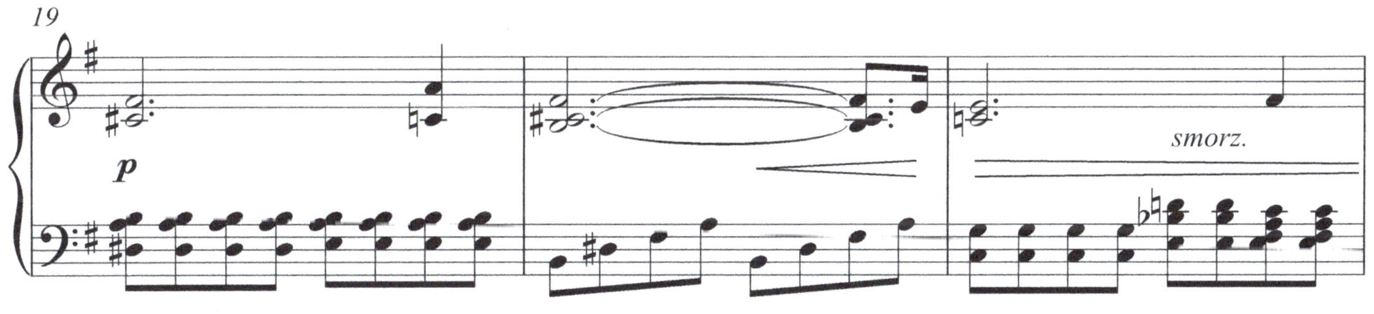
19
p
smorz.

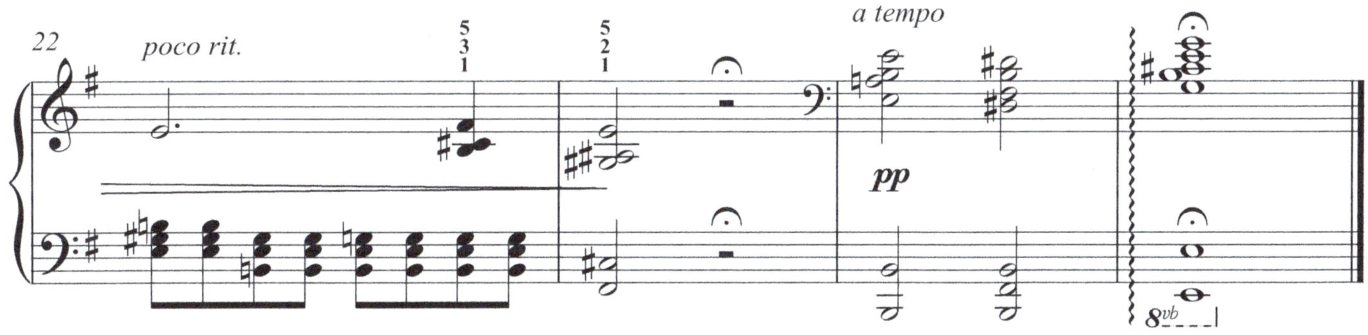
22
poco rit.
a tempo
pp
8vb

Nocturne in E♭ Major

Op. 9, No. 2

Frédéric Chopin
Arranged by Bryce Russell

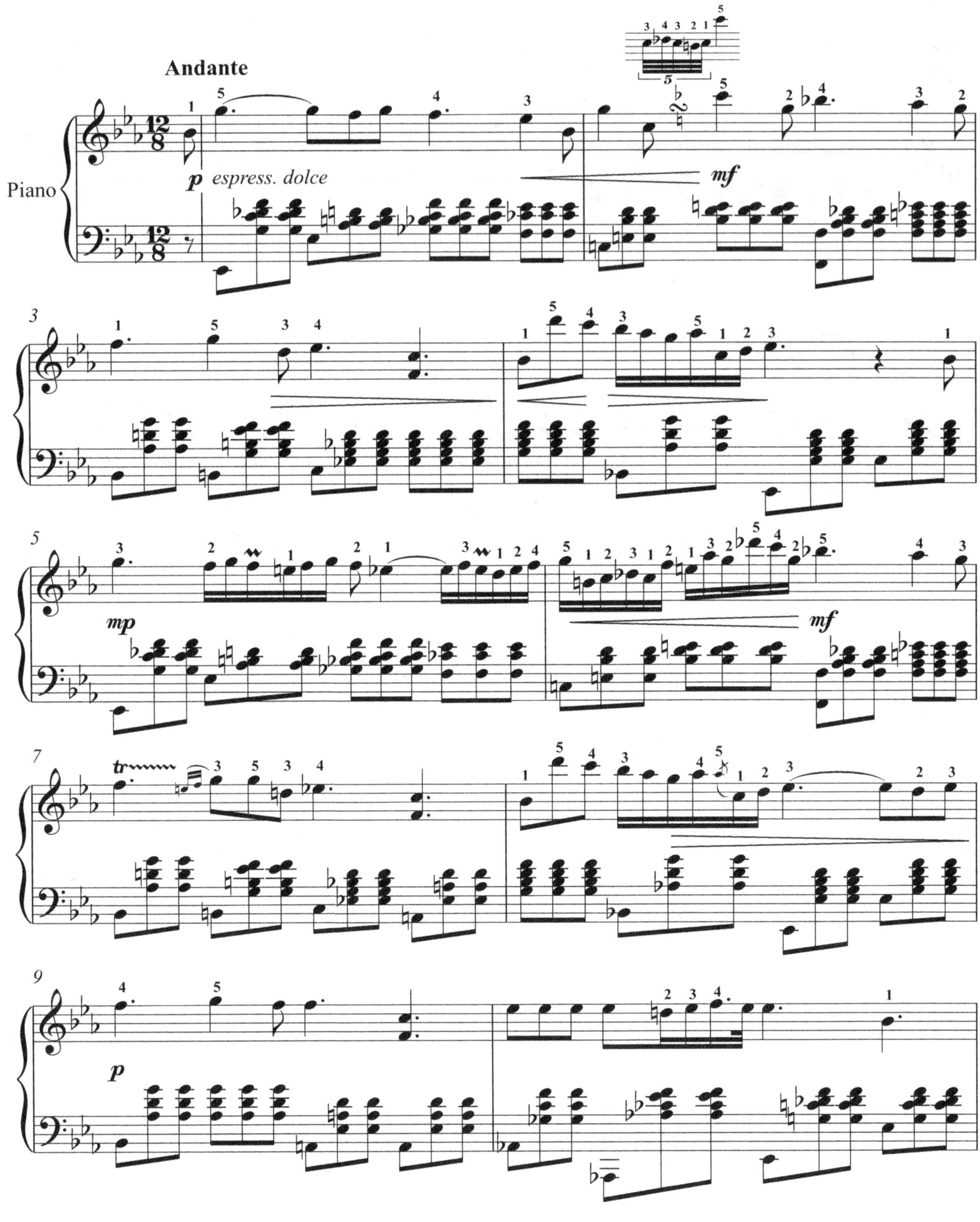

Andante

Piano

p espress. dolce

mf

mp

mf

p

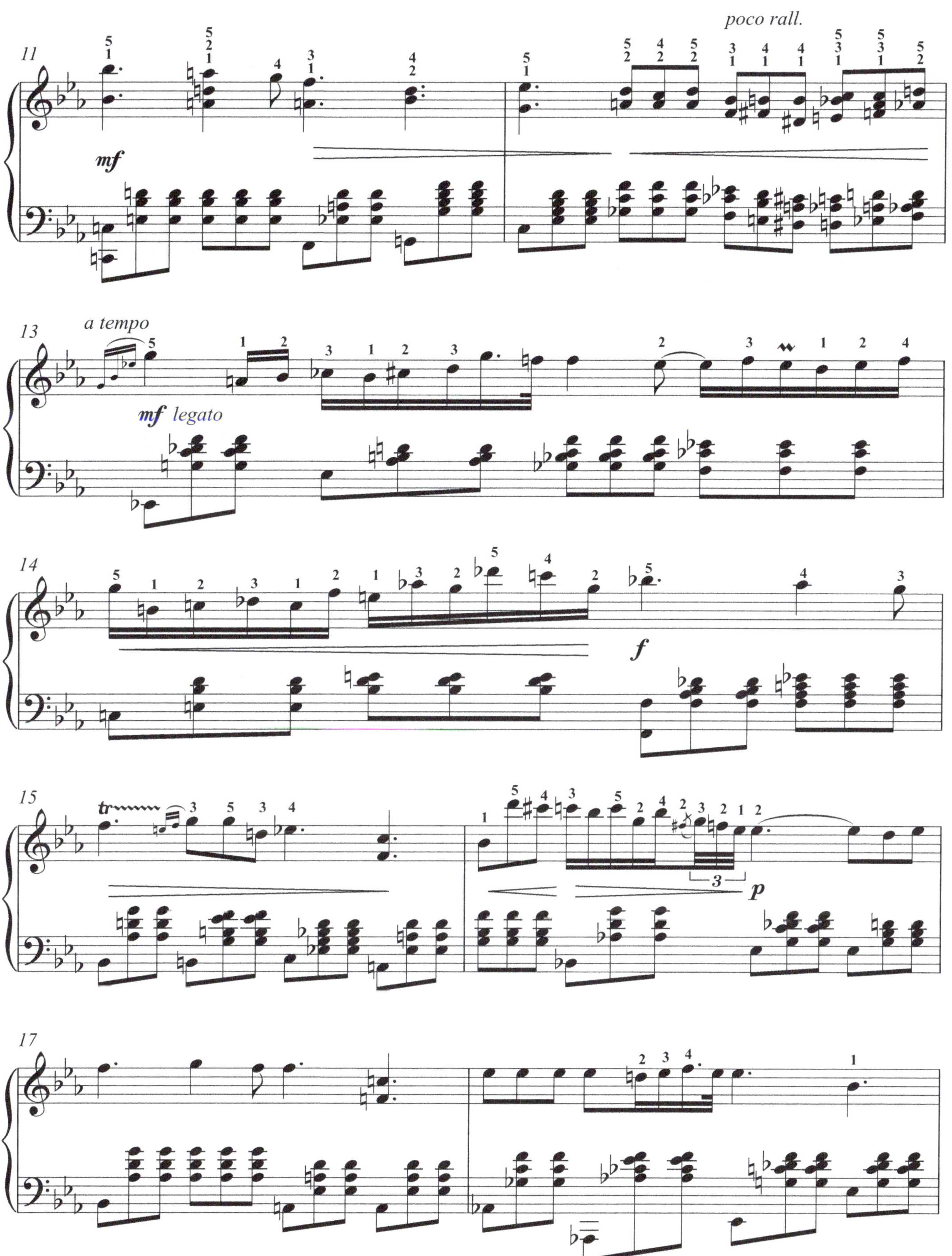
poco rall.
mf
a tempo
mf legato
f
p

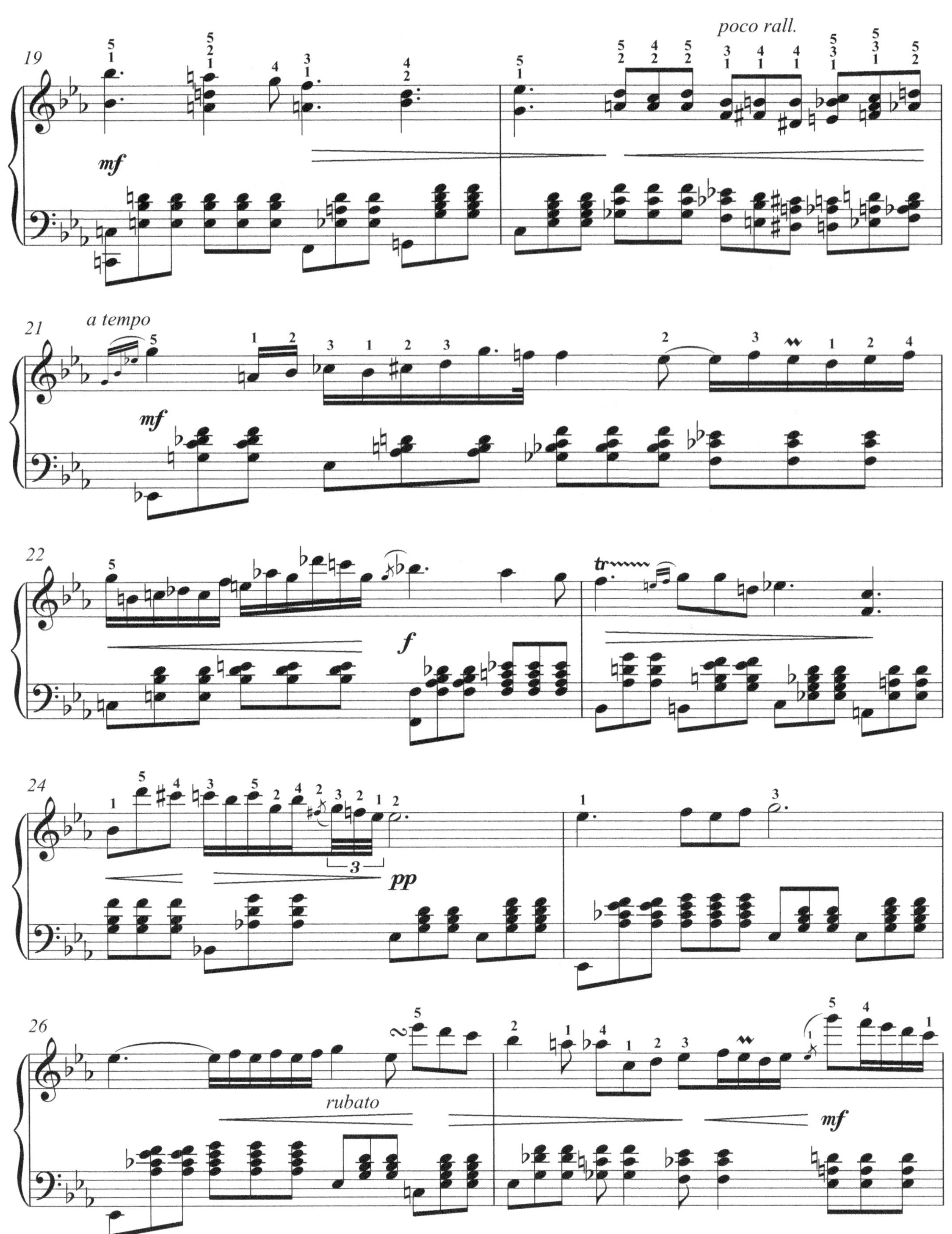
poco rall.
mf
a tempo
mf
f
pp
rubato
mf

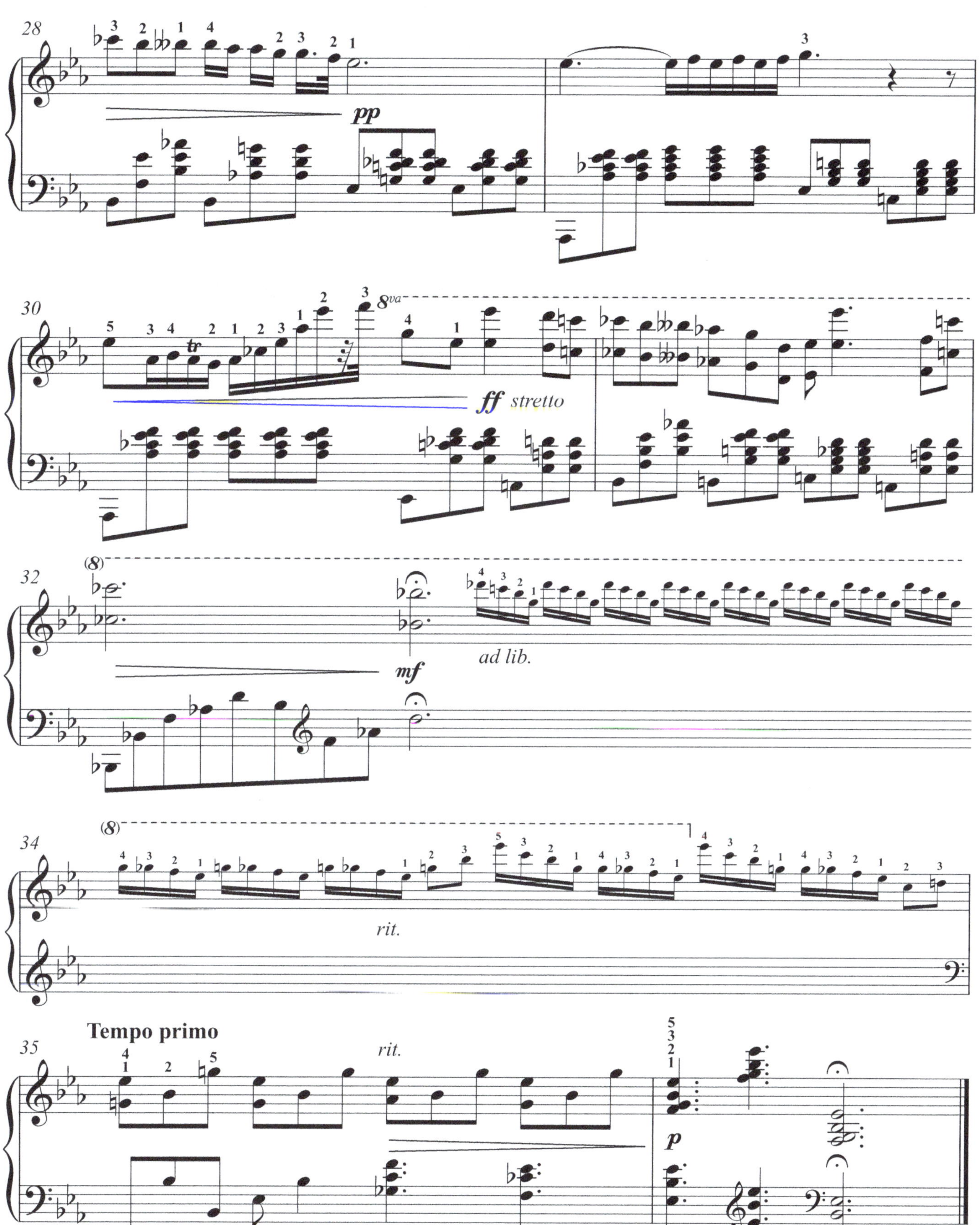
28
pp
30
8va
ff stretto
32
(8)
mf
ad lib.
34
(8)
rit.
35
Tempo primo
rit.
p

Waltz in A♭ Major

(L'adieu)

Op. 69, No. 1

Frédéric Chopin
Arranged by Bryce Russell

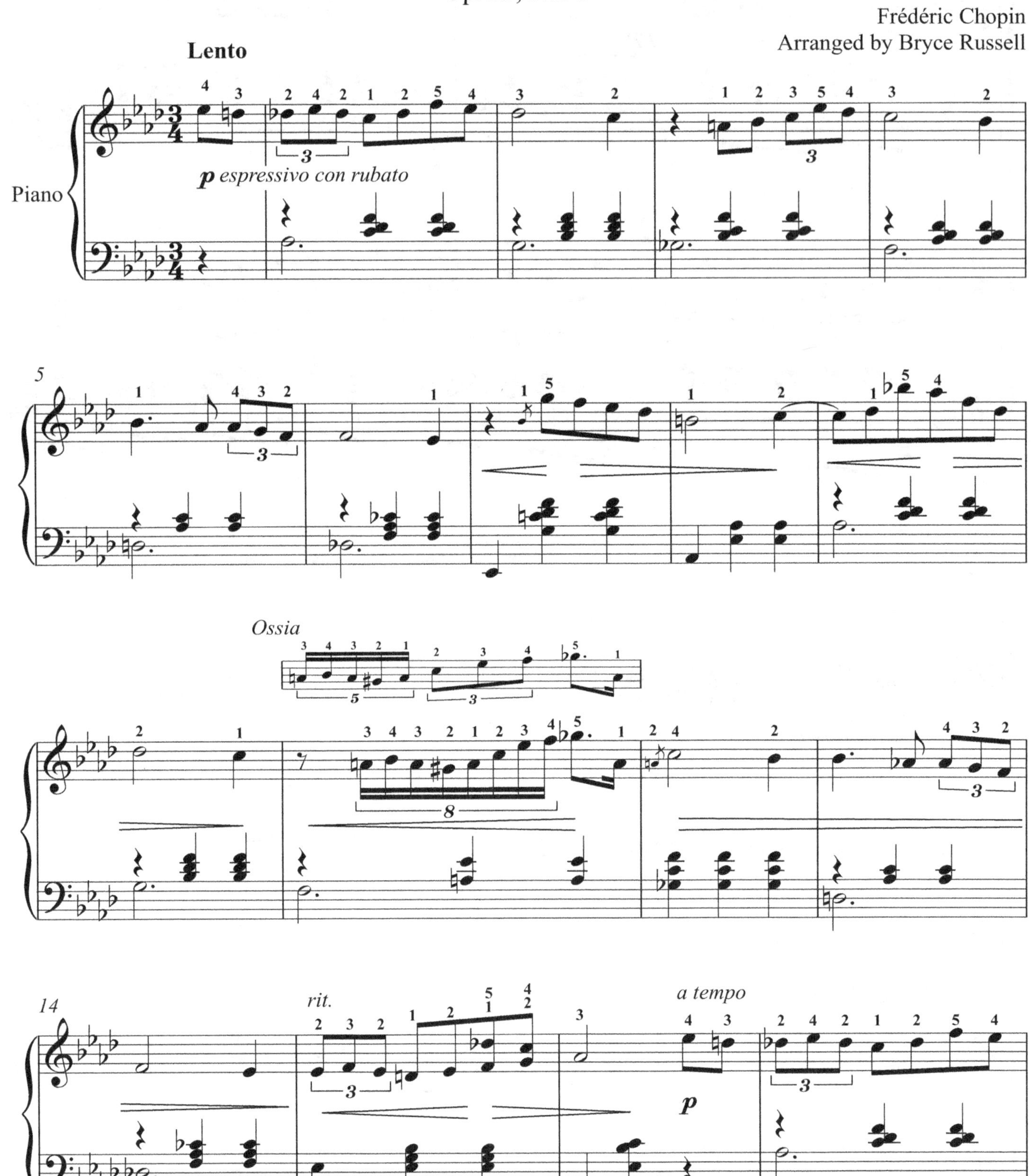

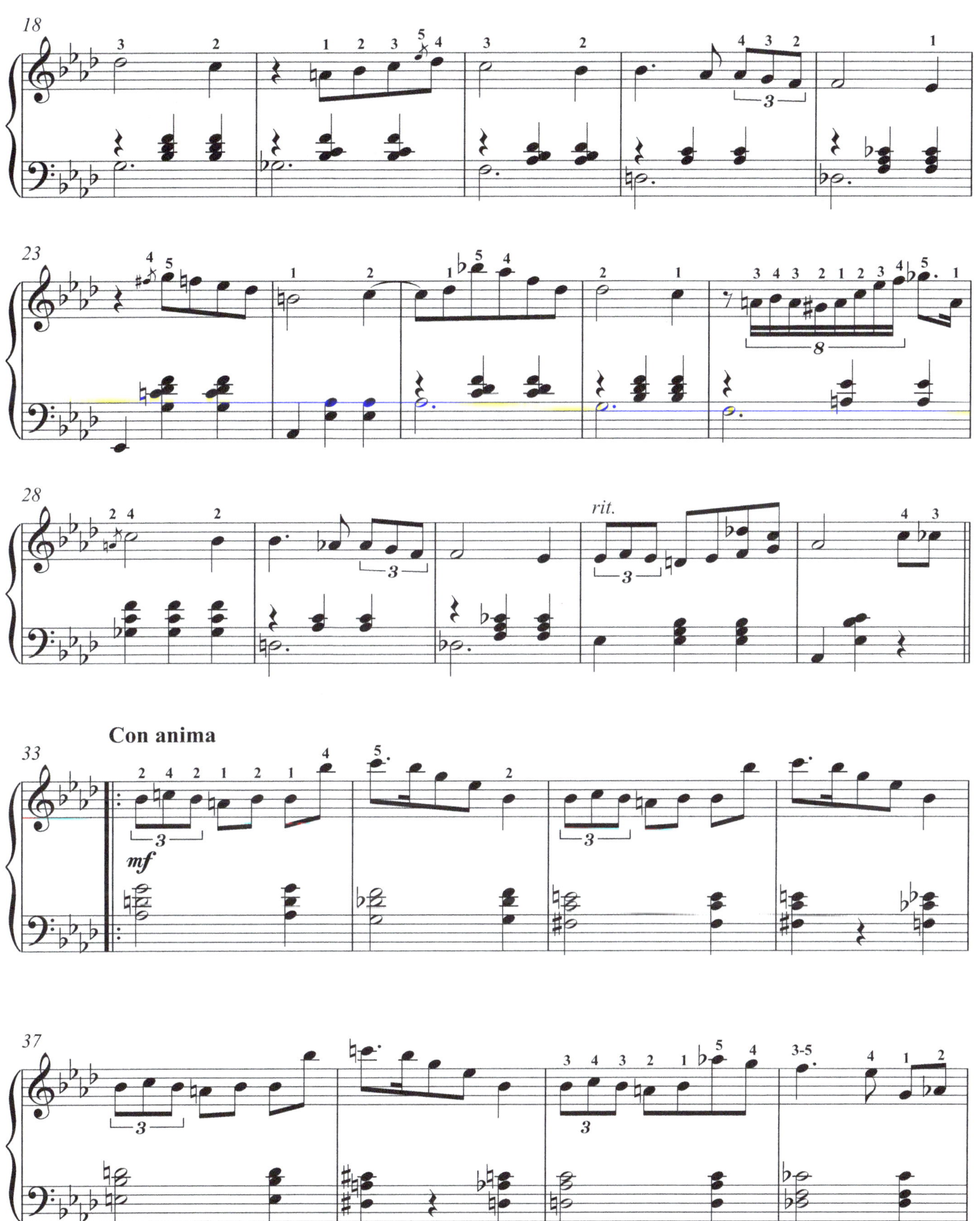

rit.
Con anima
mf

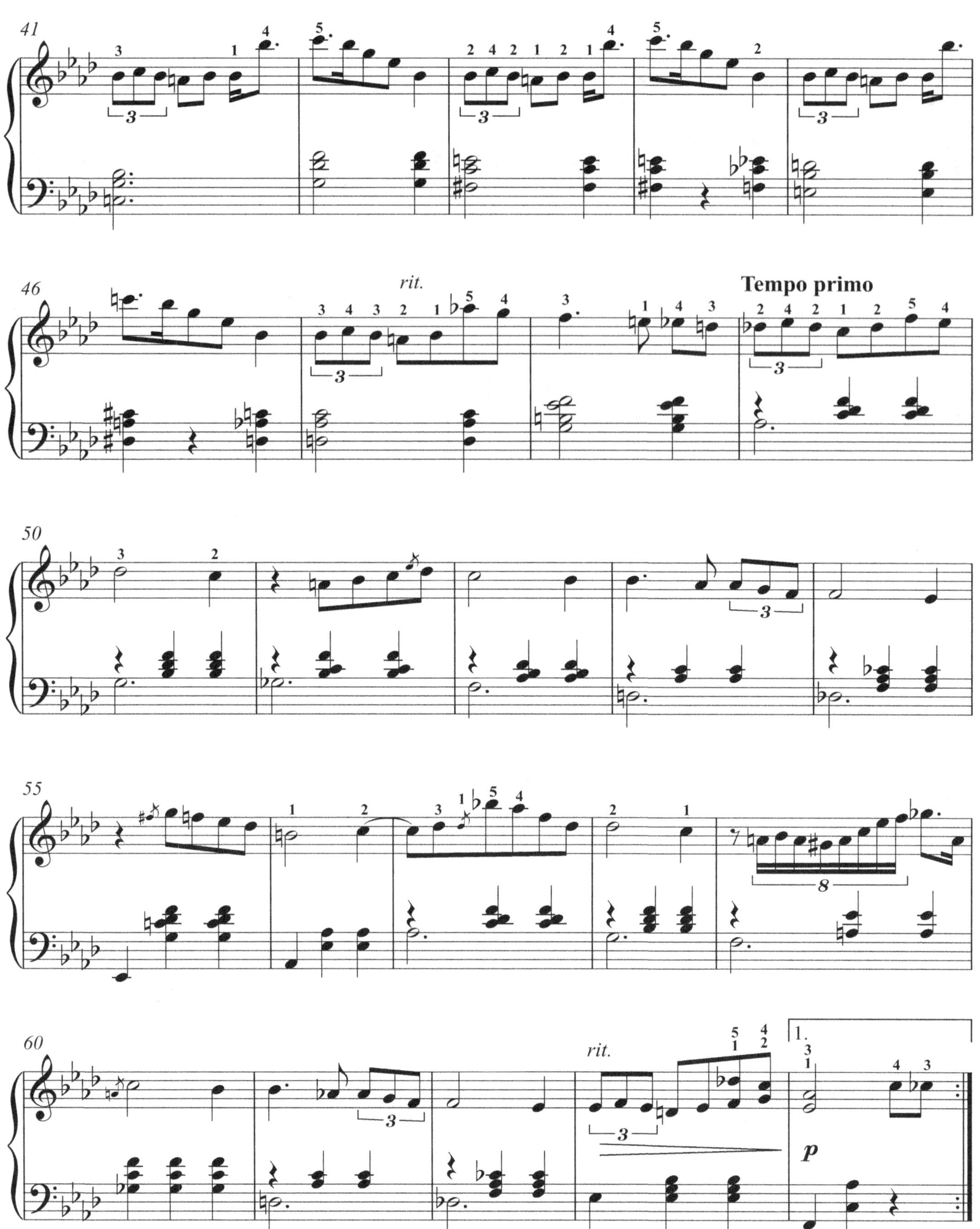
rit.
Tempo primo
rit.
p

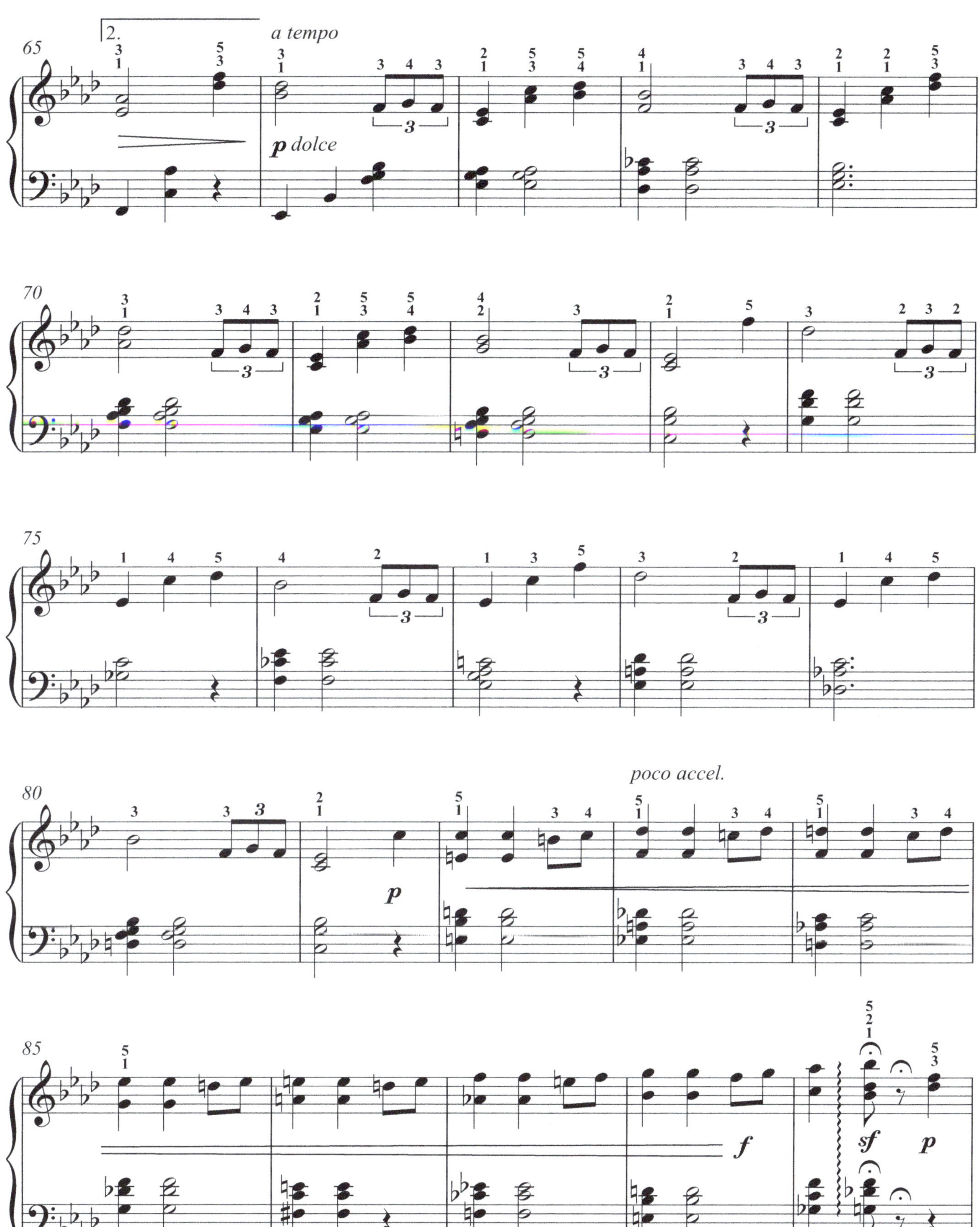
2.
a tempo
p dolce
poco accel.
p
f
sf
p

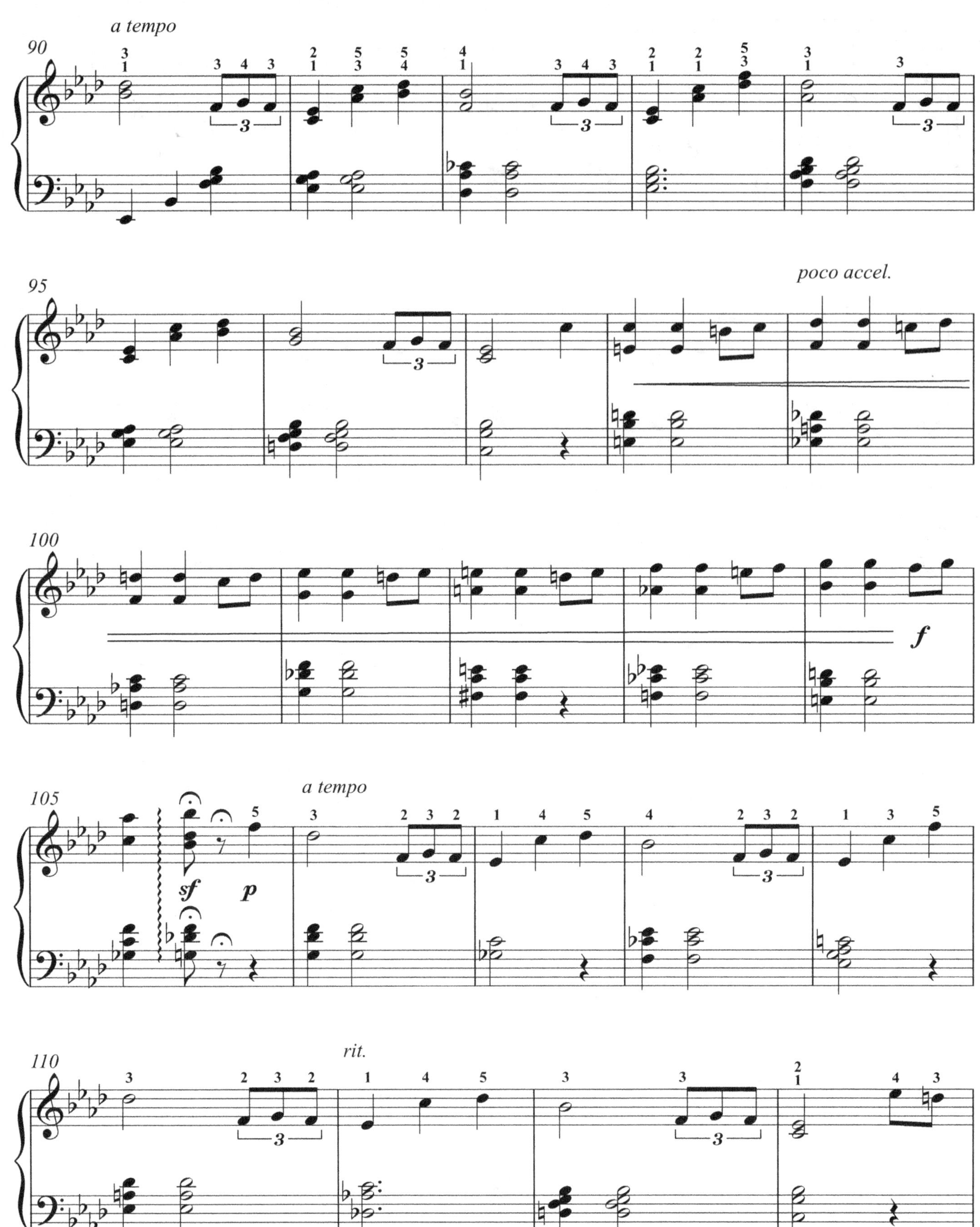
a tempo
poco accel.
f
sf
p
a tempo
rit.

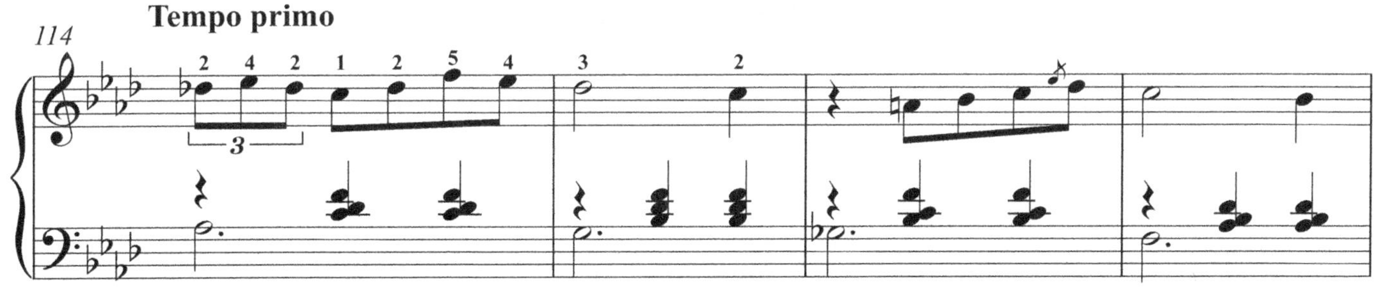
114
Tempo primo

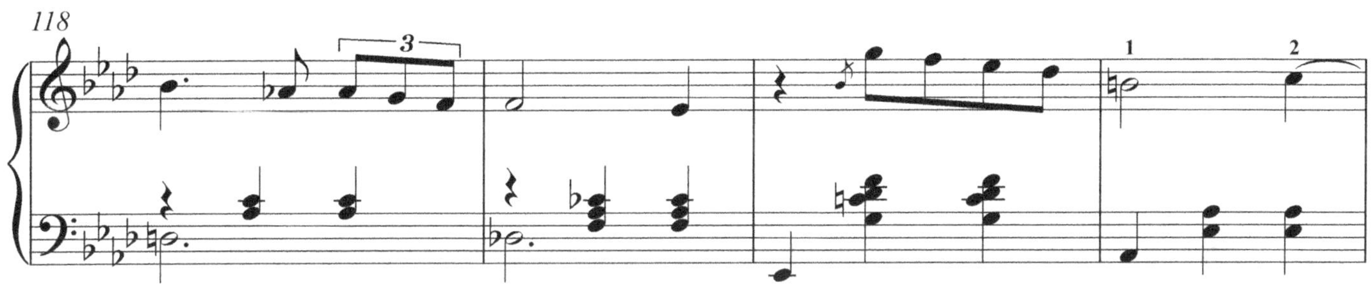
118

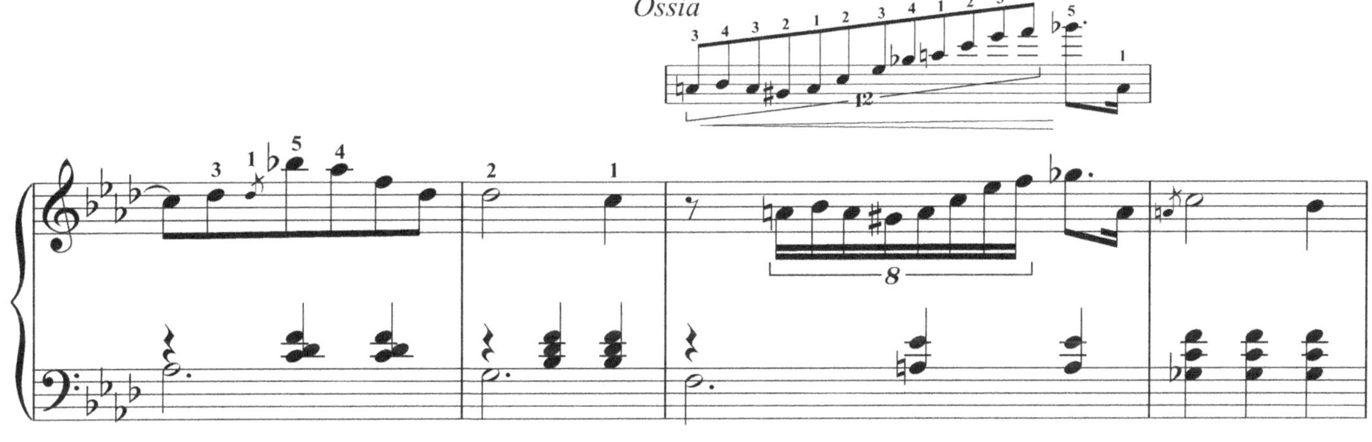
Ossia

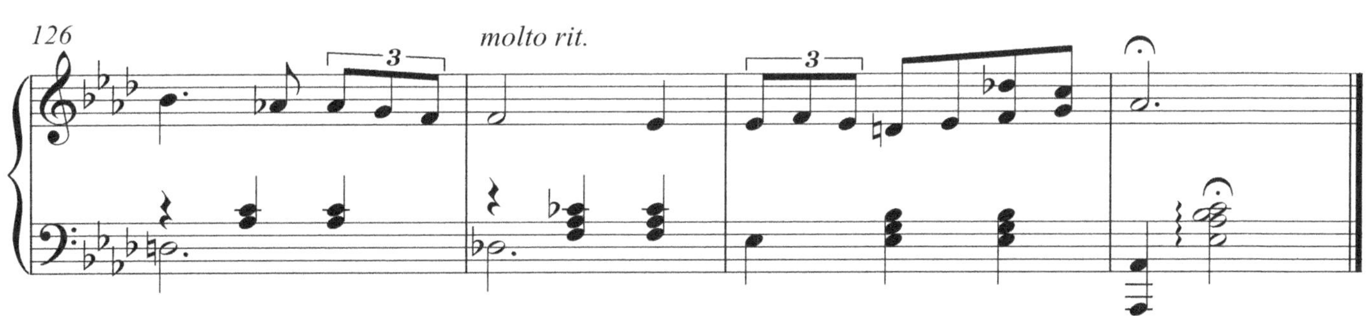
126
molto rit.

Waltz in A Minor

Posthumous

Frédéric Chopin
Arranged by Bryce Russell

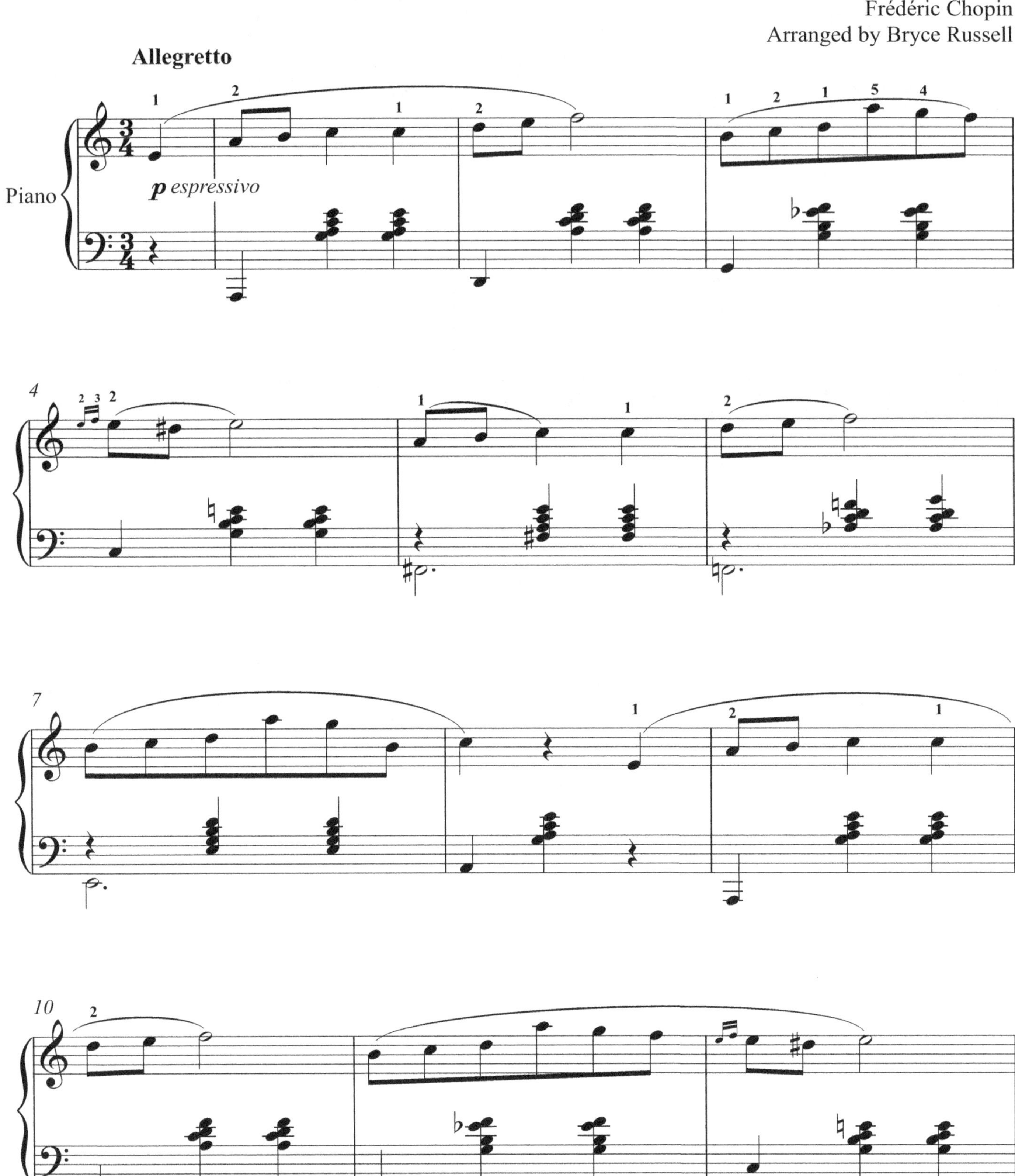

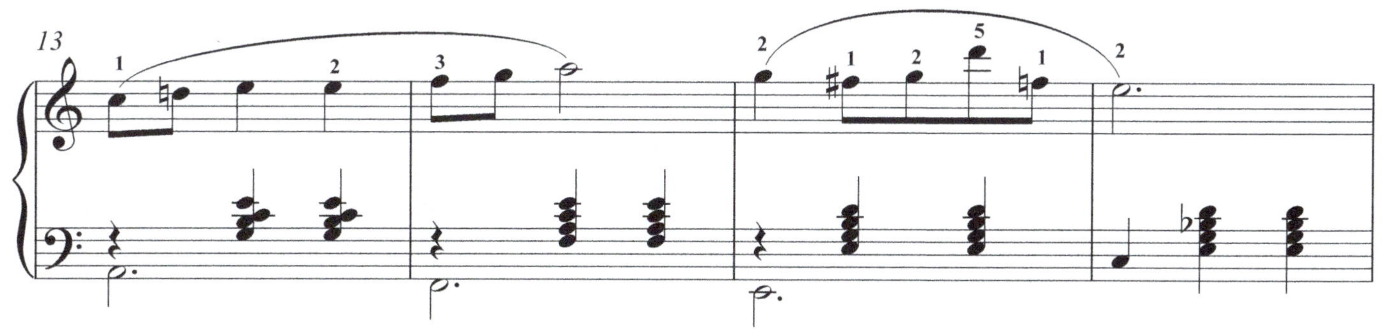
13
1
2
3
2
1
2
5
1
2
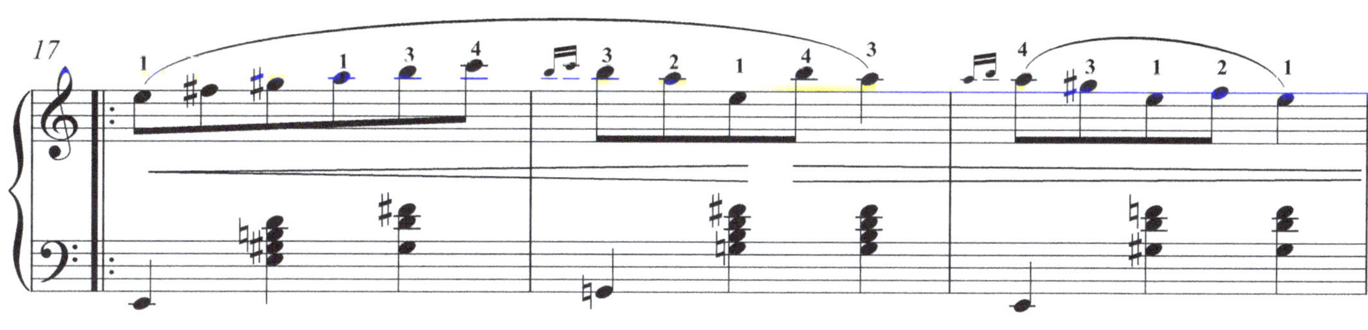
17
1
1
3
4
3
2
1
4
3
4
3
1
2
1
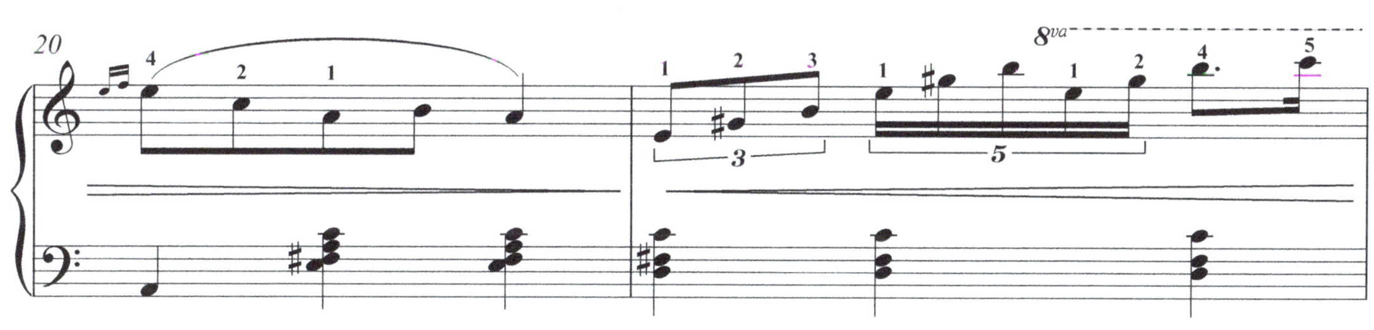
20
4
2
1
1
2
3
3
8va
1
1
2
5
4
5
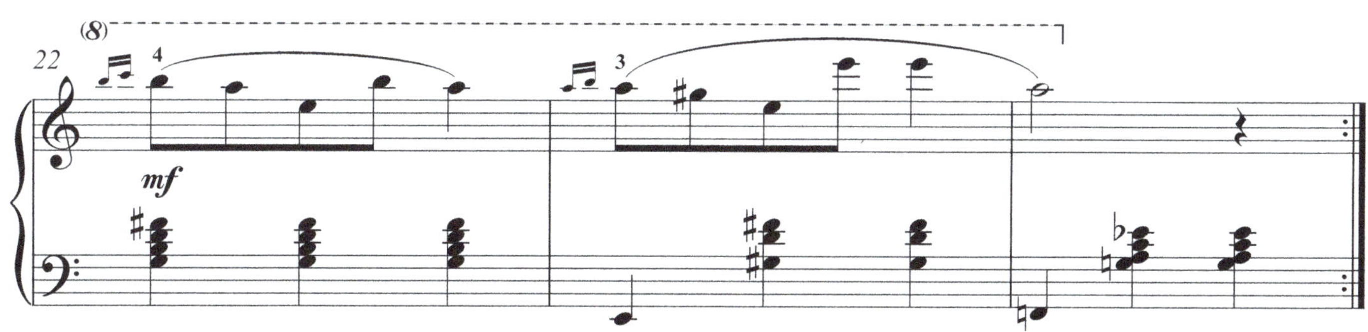
(8)
22
4
mf
3

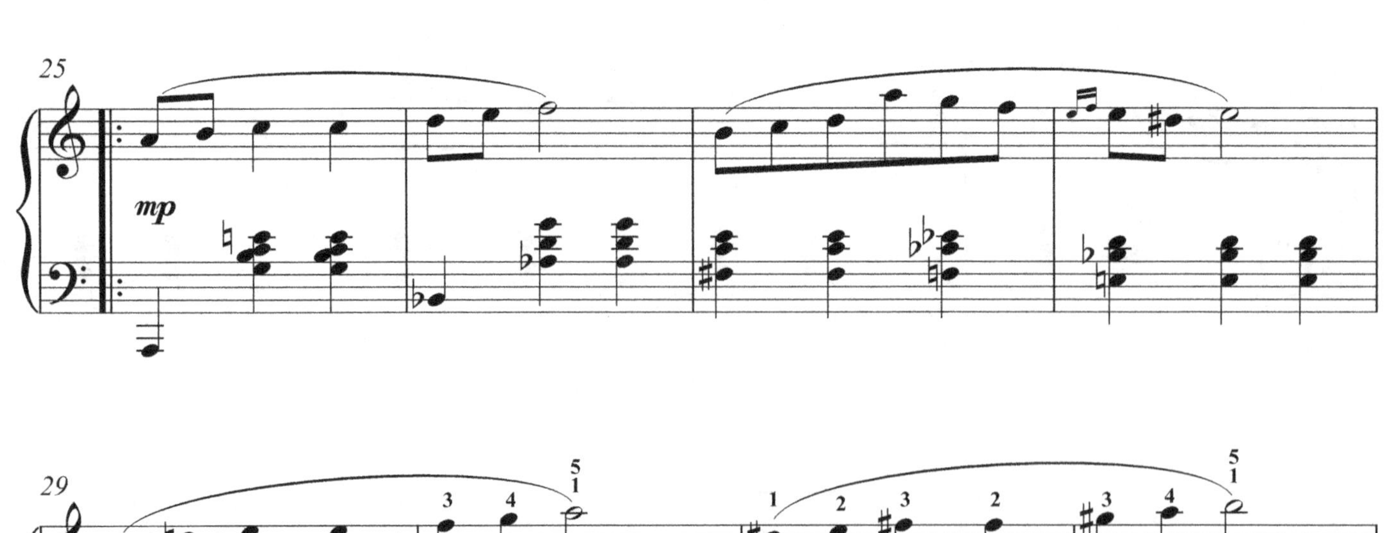
25
mp

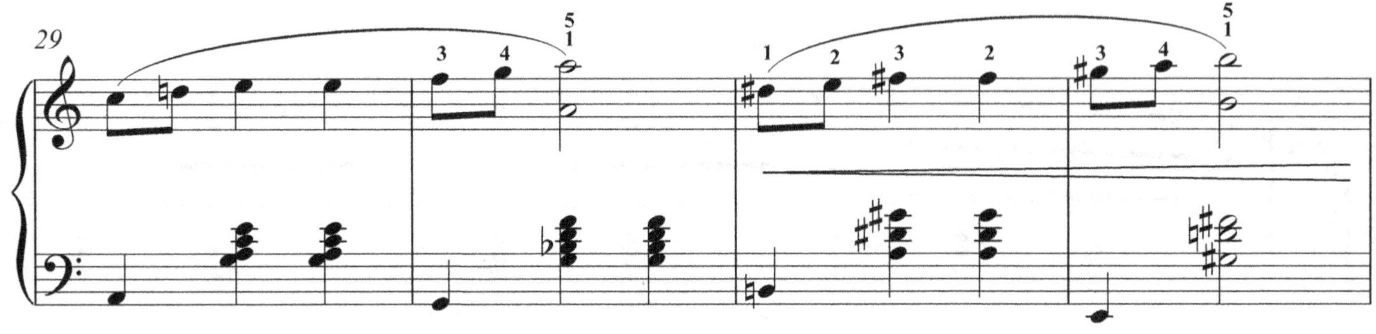
29

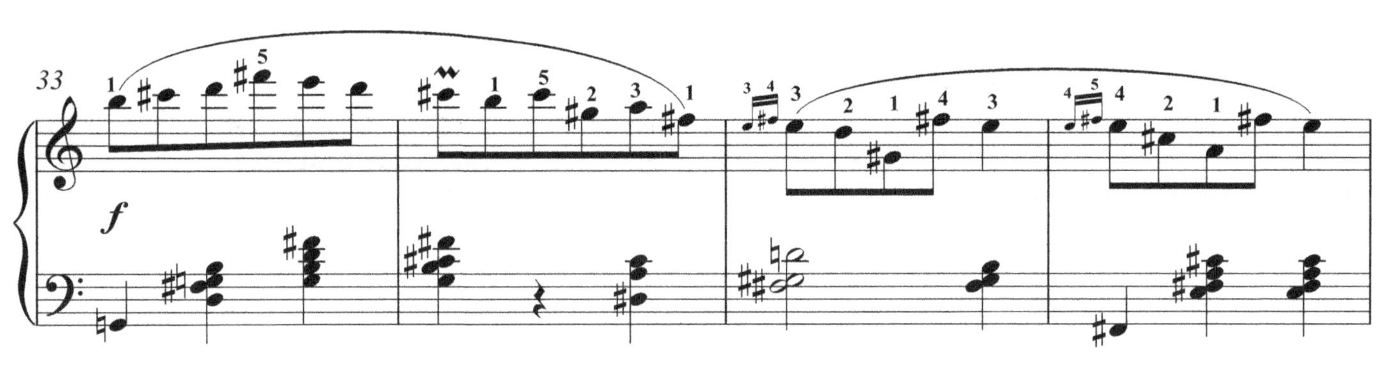
33
f

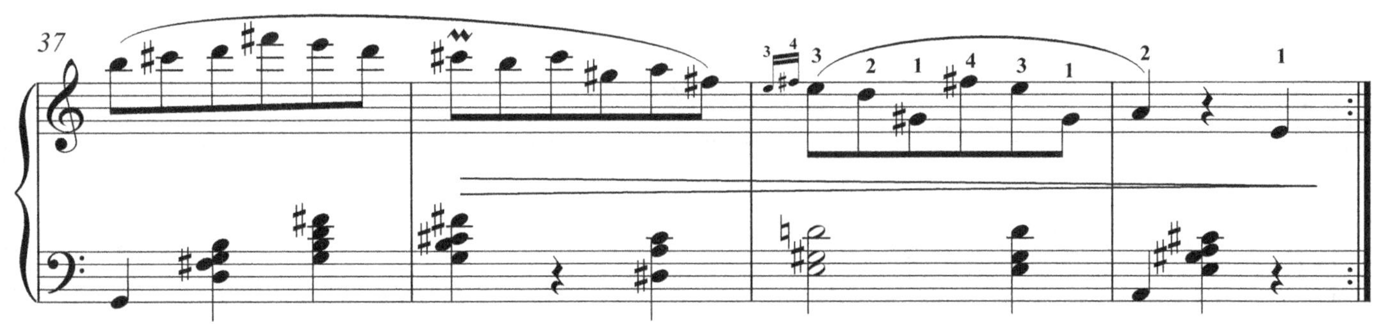
37

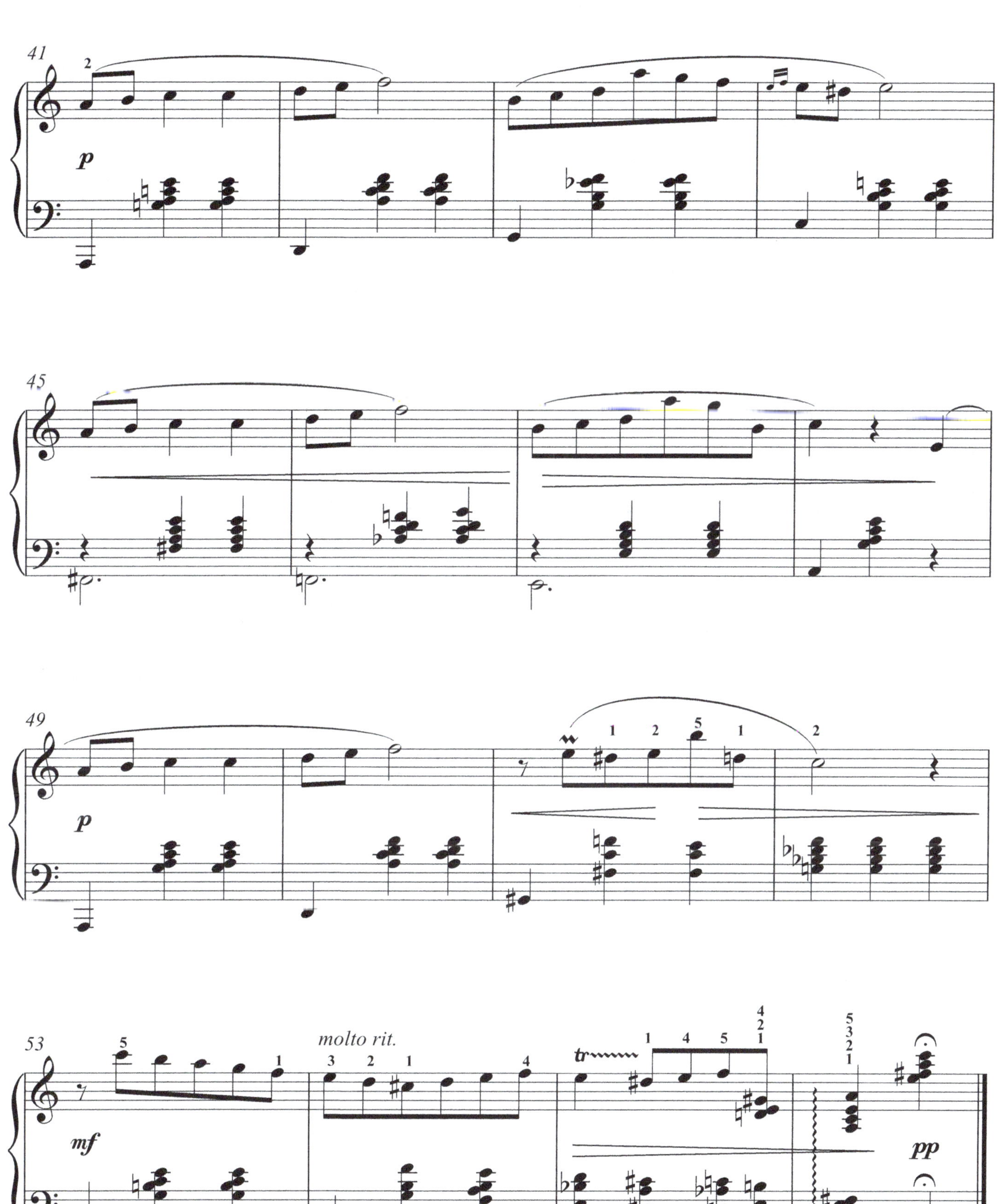
molto rit.

Waltz in B Minor

Op. 69, No. 2

Frédéric Chopin

Arranged by Bryce Russell

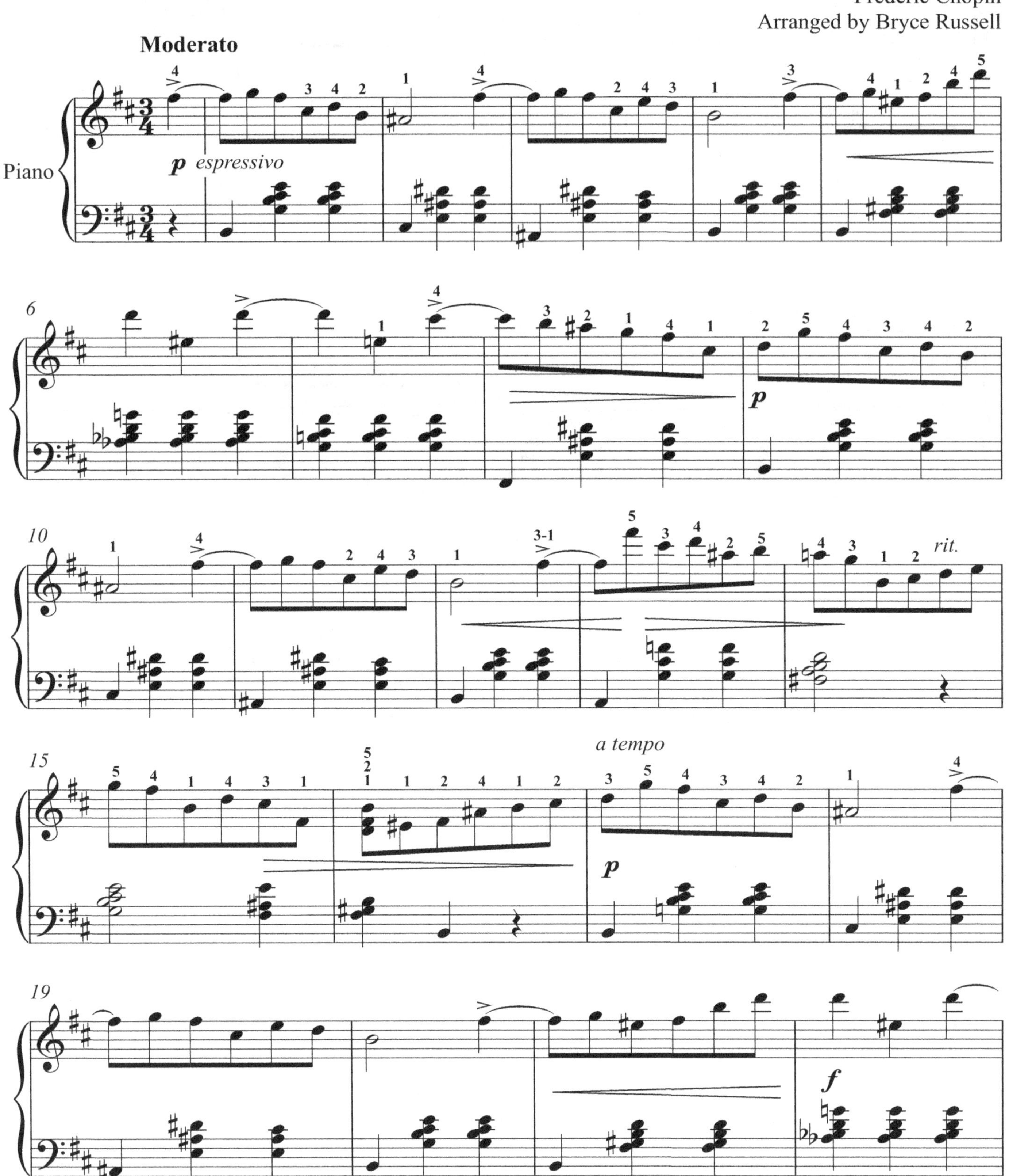

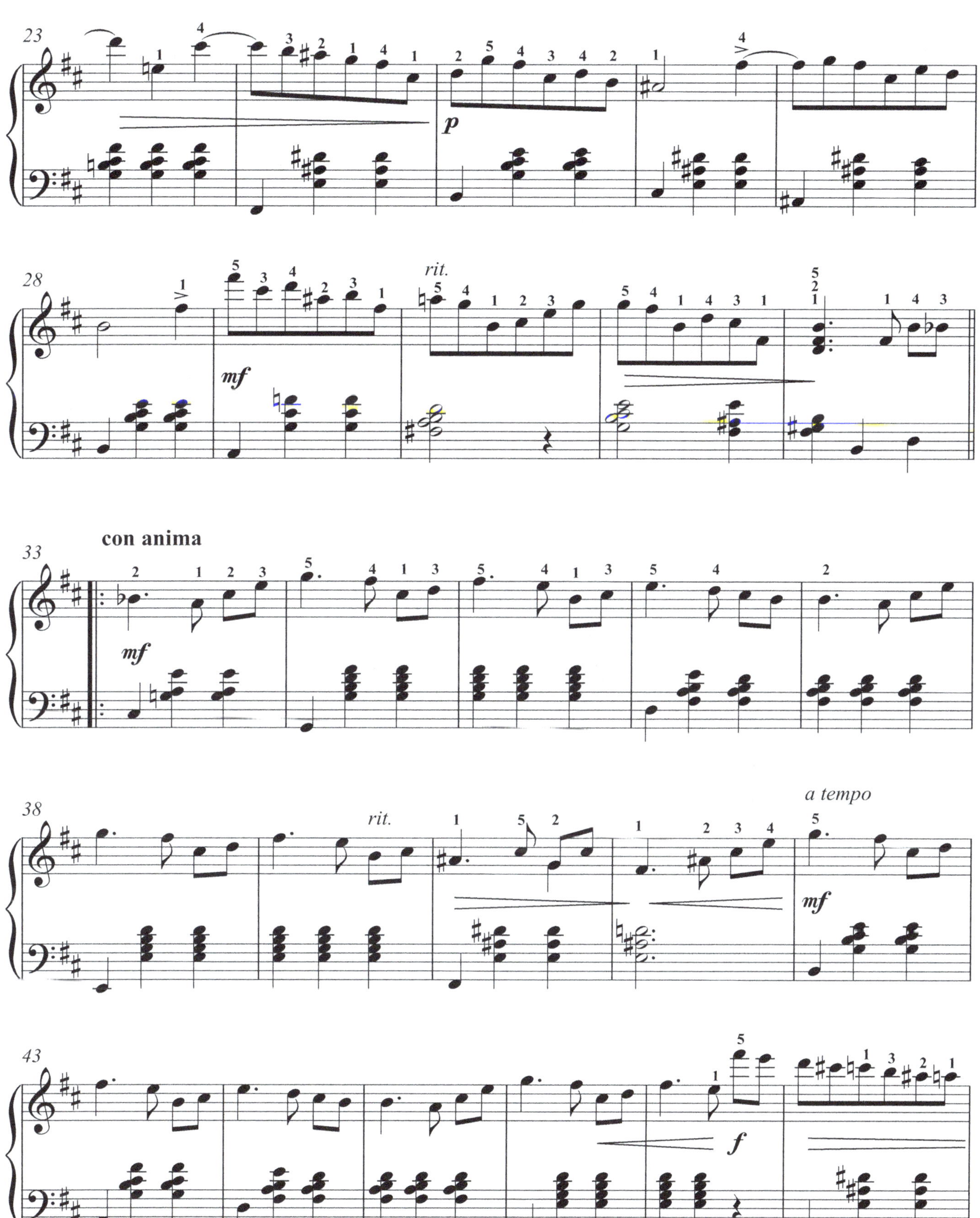
con anima
rit.
rit.
a tempo

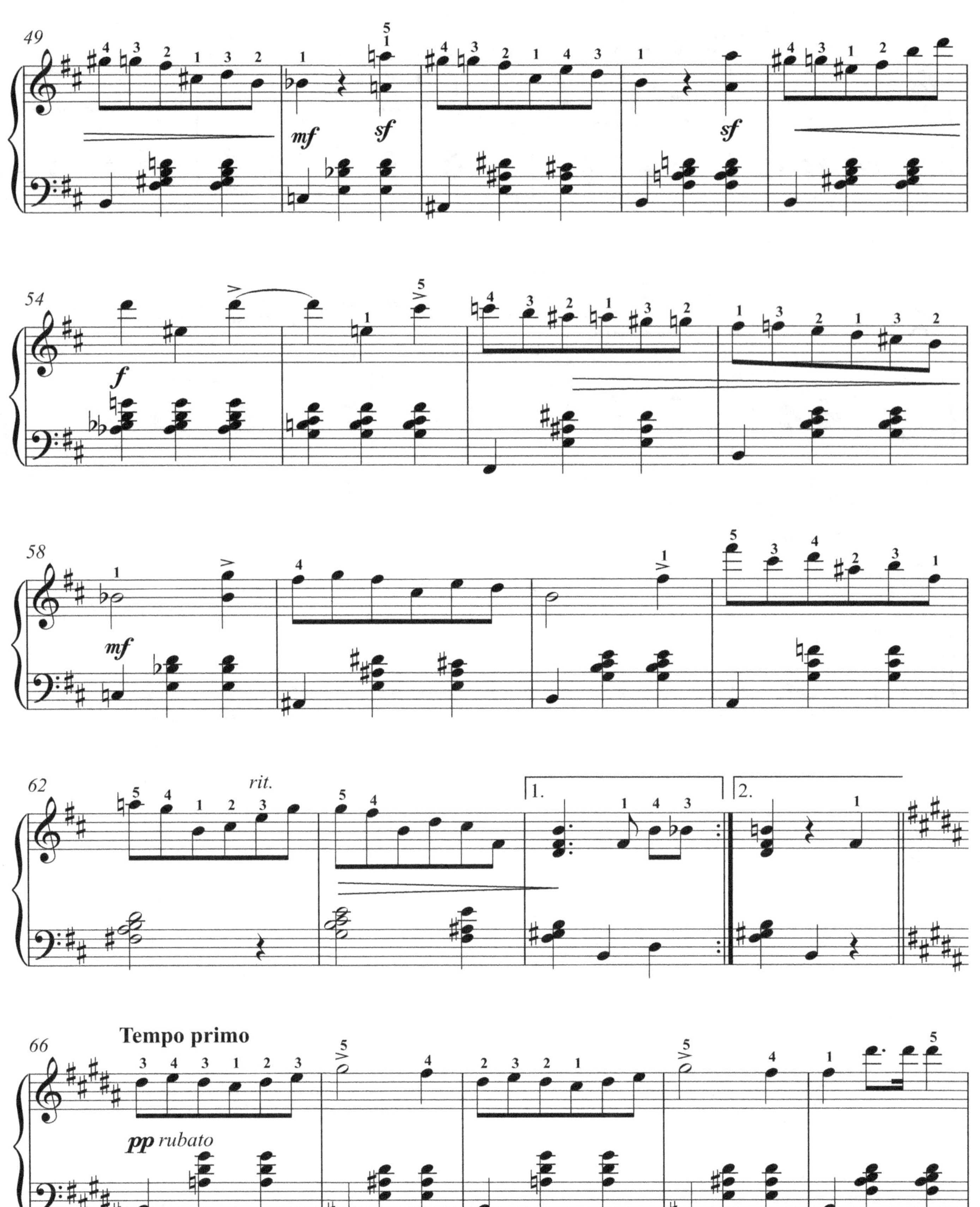
49
mf
sf
sf
54
f
58
mf
62
rit.
1.
2.
66
Tempo primo
pp rubato

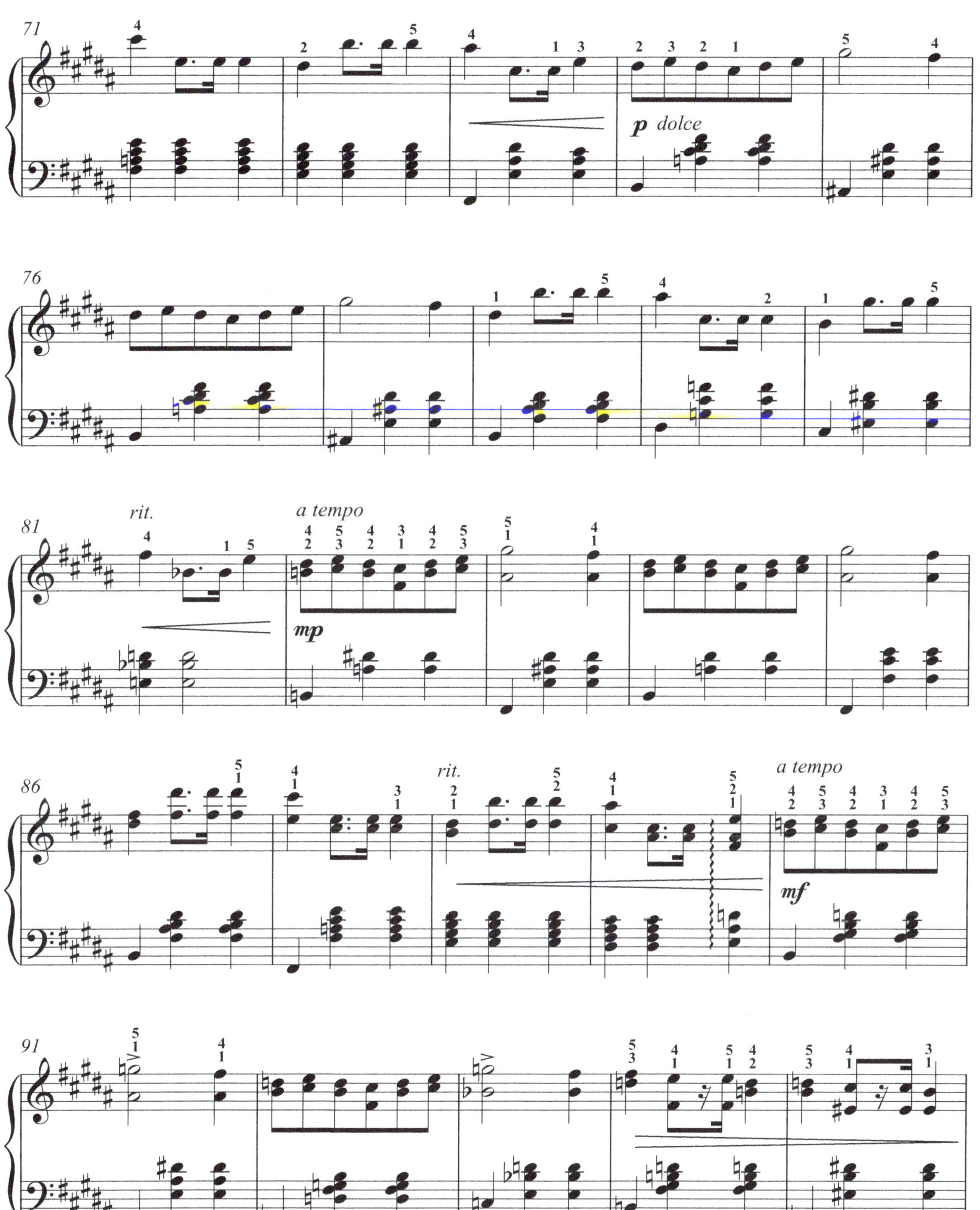

p dolce
rit.
a tempo
mp
rit.
a tempo
mf

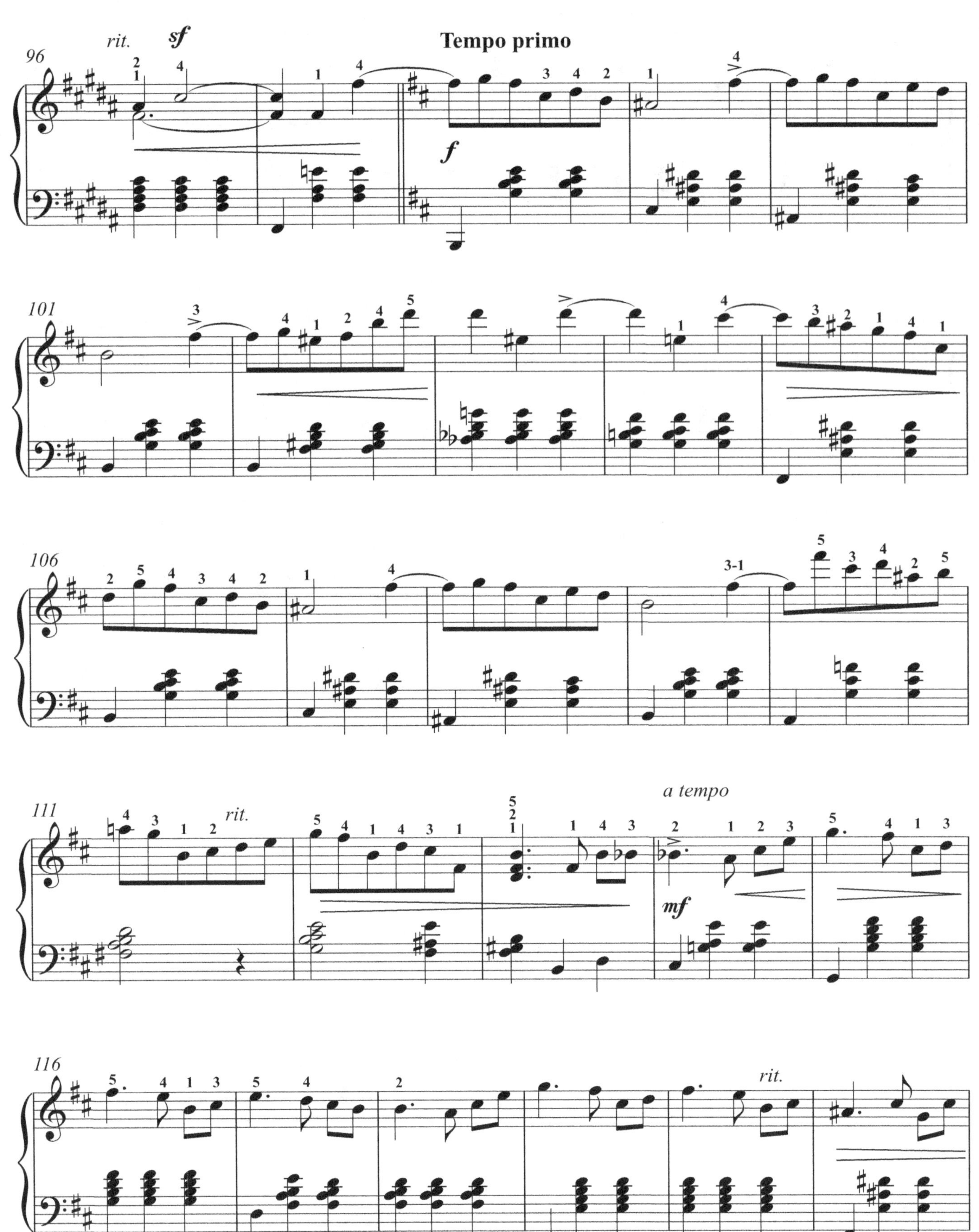
rit.
sf
Tempo primo
f
rit.
a tempo
mf
rit.

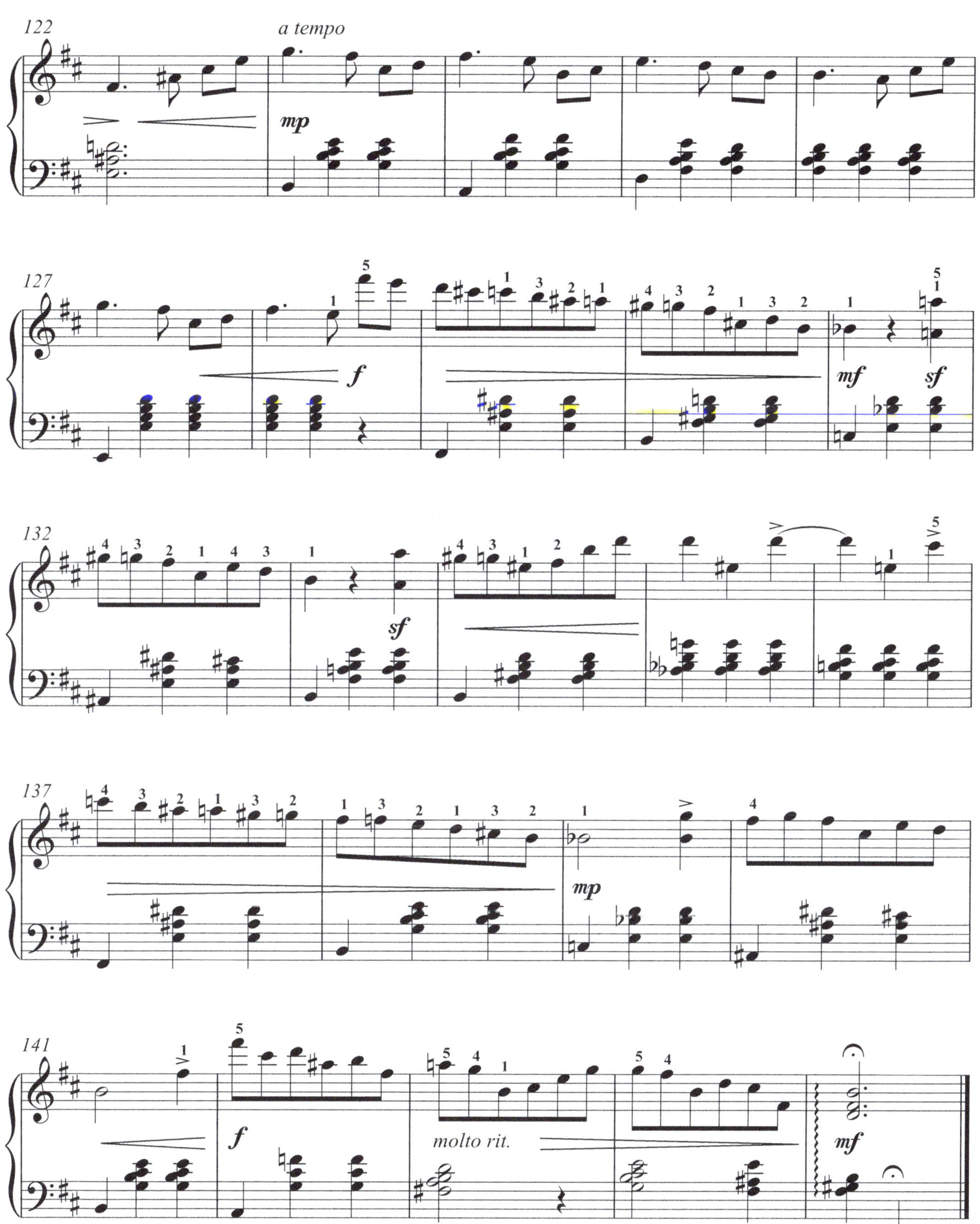
a tempo
mp
f
mf
sf
sf
mp
f
molto rit.
mf

About the Author

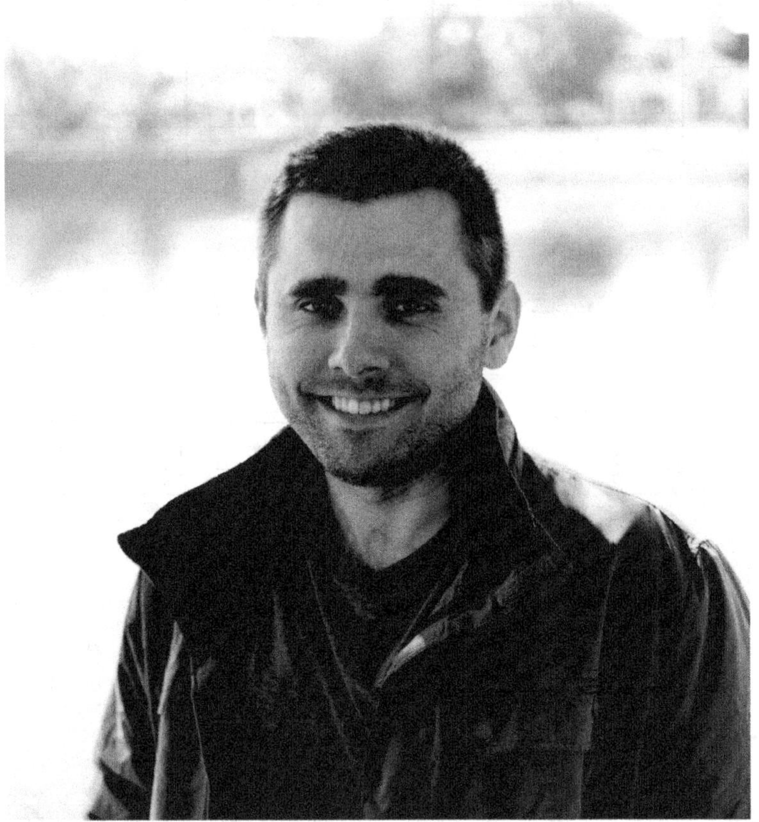

Photo by Parker Russell.

Bryce Russell is a composer, pianist, arranger, orchestrator, and author. Studied piano under Tahnia Lund and earned a Bachelor of Arts in music composition for film, television, and video games from Berklee College of Music in Boston, Massachusetts. While there, he studied with Ben Newhouse (Disney DVD logo), Vicente Avella (Family Guy & American Dad), Rick McLaughlin, Kari Juusela, and Eric Gould. He also earned a Master's degree in Curriculum and Instruction for Music with Honors (Summa Cum Laude) from Southeastern Oklahoma State University.

Russell was a member of the Music Teachers Association of California (MTAC) from 2012 to 2017. He performed original music at MTAC concerts from venues in San Diego to Oakland, CA. Another composition, "Flying with Eagles" was recognized by the city of Los Angeles with a certificate back in 2012 and an invitation to participate in the Hollywood Christmas Parade.

His music albums can be found online at Spotify and Apple Music, including his orchestral/soundtrack album *MovieScapes* (2022). Russell is currently working as a performing pianist, composer, and author.

Made in the USA
Monee, IL
09 March 2026

45112148R00031